This book was written as a
tribute to those who

serve, represent *and* **protect**

America abroad

Highways
to the
World

THE ENGINEER, THE TEACHER
AND THE DANGEROUS 20TH CENTURY

CAROLYN CALVIN KNEESE WITH JOHN DeMERS

bright sky press

HOUSTON, TEXAS

CHAPTER FRONT PHOTOS: *1 – Hard earth of Markley; 2 – Texas A&M engineering building; 3 – Texas highway workers; 4 – Elmer and his cabin; – General Leslie R. Groves; 6 – Planning Texas highways in 1950s; 7 – Earle Standlee and friends; 8 – Elmer in Egypt; 9 – Rural road in Honduras; 10 – Thai road in early 1960s; 11 – Crowded Bolivian scene; 12 – Towering ruin in Ephesus; 13 – Home on Beverly Drive.*

bright sky press
HOUSTON, TEXAS

2365 Rice Blvd., Suite 202
Houston, Texas 77005

10   9   8   7   6   5   4   3   2   1

Library of Congress Cataloging-in-Publication Data

Kneese, Carolyn, 1941-
Highways to the world : the engineer, the teacher and the dangerous 20th century / by Carolyn Calvin Kneese with John DeMers.
pages cm
ISBN 978-1-939055-44-6
1. Kneese, Carolyn, 1941—Childhood and youth. 2. Kneese, Carolyn, 1941—Family. 3. Calvin family. 4. Calvin, Elmer Ben, 1901-1997. 5. Calvin, Agnes, 1898-1994.
6. Texas--Biography. I. DeMers, John, 1952- II. Title.
CT274.C64195K64 2013
976.4'064092--dc23
2013020240

Editorial Direction, Lucy Herring Chambers
Editor, Eva J. Freeburn
Creative Direction, Ellen Peeples Cregan
Design, Marla Y. Garcia

Printed in Canada through Friesens

PRELUDE

When I was first introduced to Carolyn Kneese, she was looking for someone. Two someones, to be precise—the two most important someones in her life. Both had passed away a few years earlier. So, whether Carolyn understood it at the time or not, she was asking me to become a detective. Listening to her talk, I realized I couldn't begin to say, "No."

I could tell, from my first visit to Carolyn's home, that the detective work would not be easy. Yes, she had memorabilia gathered from her parents' long lives—letters from here or there, official contracts with foreign governments or private companies, a book of invitations to social events—many written in Thai—and of course, stack upon stack of the weathered black-and-white photos that always thrust us most directly into a time and place that's not our own. Yet not only did such materials arrive without specific shape or form, they weren't even continuous enough to form a single, uniform narrative. That would be my job, I realized a little painfully.

I also understood that I possessed even less from my late parents, who lived through these same years and appear now only in a handful of black-and-white photos I keep in a yellowed folder at my writing desk. Perhaps, I noted in some shadowy, half-forgotten corner of my brain, I might track them down after this. Or perhaps, in searching for Carolyn's parents across the mists of 20th century history, I was searching for my own at the same time.

—JOHN DEMERS

INTRODUCTION

I suspect that I knew more about my parents—about the birth of the Atomic Age with what my father simply called the "detonation device," about the beginnings of the modern Arab world with the explosions that forced my parents (and teenaged me) out of Egypt into the arms of the U.S. 6th Fleet, about the letters and postcards they wrote to me later from world hotspots like Honduras, Kuwait and even Iran—more than my mature head told me I could know. I knew it instead in long-buried memories, of a father and mother who passed through my life like adventurous, high-spirited shadows, strangers to me in so many ways, even more than all parents are strangers.

I knew it in my heart.

My small-town Texas father, Elmer Ben Calvin, is at the heart of the story. Surely, in an engineering career spanning from the 1920s into the 1970s, he was also at the heart of the dangerous 20th century. In a sense, Daddy was my own personal "Forrest Gump," always there in the foreground or at least the background, whenever and wherever history was being made. In the early years, this was the kind of history you recognize only after the fact: the golden age of Texas highways that arrived as an antidote to the Great Depression, and later as a response to America's victorious emergence from World War II. Other times, as with the Manhattan Project, the historic nature of his work was obvious to anyone who knew enough of the secrets.

From the peace that came with V-J Day to the intense Cold War that inspired and bedeviled so many of my father's projects, he was out there representing America. And that meant, to him as it would for any engineer, making a list of the problems, proposing a list of solutions and then going about the difficult work at hand.

The fact that this work took and kept him far from home is part of my family's history, just as he is now part of America's.

I also wanted to explore a darker dimension of my father's life, one perhaps best expressed by his younger brother Bob, who spent his entire life close to the family's roots in rural Texas. "Going to someplace like Ankara for a year and building *one mile* of highway?" cousin Janis Cravens remembers her father exaggerating. "Elmer was always in some hotspot, right before there was a revolution or some kind of coup. We always suspected Elmer was doing *something* for the government." My family had a lot of theories about what that "something" was. As Janis recalls to this day: "Every time my father would see Elmer off, he said he wasn't sure he'd ever see him again."

Only now, looking back from the 21st century, can I fully recognize what a remarkable woman my mother was. A school teacher from a small town who taught mostly in other small towns, she would also teach in countries so remote from an older, simpler America that few of her original students could have found them on a map. Coming before the birth of mass tourism in the 1960s, this meant headaches and heartaches with language, with culture, with food and other details of daily life that, in all but the most closed-off geographies, have now cured themselves.

No matter where I go today, no matter what I do, I can't replicate what it must have been like for my mother in the places she traveled with my father for work. The trips she and I took together, apart from that work and the global struggles that gave it form, are not only fond memories. They are flashes of striking clarity about distant times and places. To tell this story properly, I also had to uncover the history of my Uncle Earle, my mother's brother. Earle Standlee passed through my family's life time and again, and not just during the holidays. As medical leader for America's forces when they swept across Europe toward Berlin, and later as Surgeon General in postwar Japan, Earle represented the "better angels" that our country sends forth. The fact that his job as a doctor promised he would do everything in his power to heal is only right in a world, indeed in a century, that cried out for so much healing.

For me, beginning to research and write the first chapter of my parents' journey seemed both love poem and detective story. There's so little we know about our parents, really—whether they lived caught up in historical events or a thousand miles from the nearest one. One moment they are with us, ready to be asked, "Can you tell me about the time…," and then the next moment, they are gone. All we have then is a handful of remembered—or sometimes misremembered—impressions, points on the compass of their lives, where we might meet them if we're willing to wait long enough. In that sense, this *is* detective work: placing ourselves on a long-forgotten street corner, in hopes that on a certain day at a certain hour our parents will walk past, younger than they have any right to be, bursting with a life we never knew.

That's our assignment, in the great, long relay race between our parents and our children, each of us with the briefest of moments to hold the baton. As children, to borrow the one phrase my parents and their entire generation understood better than any other, that's our job.

TWO ROADS
Diverged

CHAPTER ONE

One of my strongest memories of my father is also one of my last. He was past ninety by this time, and understandably a mere shadow of the strong, tall Texas military man and engineer he had once been. We often went to visit the old "home place" (now known as Brushy Creek Ranch) in Markley, a town that *wasn't* one, simply the intersection of two roads-less-traveled where the memory of Fort Worth gazes across rugged Young County to the long-ago western frontier. Elmer Ben Calvin had spent only brief pockets of time in Markley since his childhood, whether he was living with my mother and me in Austin or Dallas, in

→ *Elmer at age 4*

World War II's "secret city" of Oak Ridge, Tennessee, or in foreign countries as diverse as Egypt, Honduras, Colombia, Bolivia, Turkey, Kuwait and Iran. Yet somehow to him, almost mysteriously as I came to learn that day, Markley remained his home.

At some point, as we strolled across land that had remained in my family since the late 1800s, Daddy bent over unexpectedly. At his age, of course, such a thing was frightening. But as I looked on, all my father did was gather some of the Markley soil into his age-twisted hands and hold it there, slowly pressing his fingers through it. When he finally lifted his body upright, there were tears glistening in his eyes.

At that moment, I couldn't say for sure what Elmer Calvin was crying about—whether it was the happy times he'd had on this land so many decades earlier, whether he was missing my mother who had preceded him in death, or whether he was thinking of Calvins he'd known here growing up, who'd played some formative role in his undeniably remarkable life. He had traveled so long and so far from these two diverging country roads, roads that in his memory were dusty in dry spells and muddy after a rain, hard to get very far either way. "Where did they lead?" he must have wondered as a young boy here. Did they really lead anywhere? Few of his family had made it past Graham, the Young County seat, or even past Jacksboro, a place his elders sometimes took him to market. Surely these roads went farther than that. For him, they just *had* to.

Today, those acres in Markley remain in the family. The elementary school my father attended is closed, the Baptist church my family helped start is gone too. I think of Markley as more of a cemetery than anything else, a beloved place we'd go each year in the spring to spruce up, respectfully wiping the gravestones and hauling off rotting branches and fallen leaves. Cemetery Decoration Day, we called it through the decades, and everybody around Markley who was able to help decorate would come. In keeping with their globetrotting lives, my parents are not buried in this small patch of earth in the middle of Texas nowhere. Yet in some way, here alongside my father's parents and grandparents, all of us Calvins are buried, residing in this place forever.

Elmer Ben Calvin was born in Markley on August 14, 1901, and as at other moments in his life and career, the man's timing was uncanny. Almost in salute to his international future, Young County welcomed its first true link to modernity that very same year. The Rock Island Line started making stops in

Graham, the local *Leader* trumpeted in large extra-bold headlines with exclamation points that were usually reserved for war or peace. "IT HAS COME!" the paper crowed. "GRAHAM IS CONNECTED WITH THE OUTSIDE WORLD BY BANDS OF STEEL!"

Part of those headlines was pure gloating, naturally, but part had to be relief. After all, the *Leader* seemed to be, over the decades, one of the few entities around that saw a future for the self-proclaimed Gem City of the West. There had been misses since the town was founded by two brothers, Edwin Smith and Gustavus Adophus Graham, in 1872, literally "missing" the town by miles. Everybody knew, for instance, that the Texas and Pacific would pass through town eventually—but it never got closer than sixty miles. And then everybody was sure about the Forth Worth and Denver, until it veered an equal distance to the north.

As late as the start of the 20th century, a railroad known as the Weatherford, Mineral Wells and Northwestern had contracts in place but seemed in no hurry to lay track; but then the deal with the Rock Island Line was struck. With virtually the entire town out to celebrate, the first track reached Graham's new depot on September 30, 1902. Others got the message after that, with the Wichita Falls arriving when my father was six and the Gulf, Texas and Western when he was eight. In between those arrivals, the town and the county surrounding it enjoyed its first-ever economic boom. And my father experienced the earliest memory he ever shared with me.

"About 1906 or 1907, Grandpa invited me, age five or six, to go with him to Jacksboro," he told me, his voice by this time feeble with age. "In a one-horse buggy, arriving after dark and going to the wagon yard—no, not a motel." For motels to exist there had to be highways, something my father would someday have a whole lot to do with. "After feed and stall for the horse and a bed for us, we each had a can of tomatoes and a few crackers.

→ *Brushy Creek Ranch in Markley*

Grandpa took me down to the railroad depot. He held me on his shoulders so I could look inside a passenger car."

Sometimes, I think, so much of our later lives is right there before us, as it was that evening for this child with no reason to think he'd ever travel more than twenty or thirty miles from his own home. If only we knew how to recognize it.

Good times came to Young County in 1907, at least relative to the times it had before, thanks initially to a rare event in farming: an excellent harvest that could be sold at excellent prices. A full thirty-one thousand bales of cotton were sold in Graham that year. So many outsiders came to the town to cash in that they ended up sleeping in the courthouse as well as the new train depot. The town itself voted to enlarge its boundaries, with many new commercial buildings rising within them. And within a couple years of all this activity, cattle ranching became popular as well. World War I (and much later World War II) increased the market for beef several times over, and Young County's cattlemen were more than happy to keep the supply coming.

Good times or bad, Markley sits at the very northeastern tip of Young County, where Archer and Jack counties seem about to collide. Today, of course, you might wonder why the place has an official name at all, but like a lot of towns in Texas, it used to be bigger than it is now.

It was at first merely a settlement, a place with a few small hand-built houses clustered together among the plum groves for mutual protection—this was the Texas frontier, after all. And that explains why Plum Grove was both its original name and a phrase that has turned up over and over, including on the Baptist church my family helped organize with nine members in 1888. Things started happening here after the Civil War, right around the time J.C. Calvin was settling in. One Mr. Smith built a cotton gin, which both reflected and encouraged the raising of that particular crop. Very little had been grown commercially around Markley before that, so the cotton gin got things moving.

The settlement got its own post office in 1888 and the new name Manlee. But that name lasted only a few years, the place becoming Markley in honor of General A.C. Markley, who commanded military posts at the western edge of what was then considered civilization. Among the early townspeople was W.J. Wright, who ran a general store in the town for thirty-six years while serving as postmaster for more than half of that. Doing what you had to—that was always part of life for the older people Elmer Calvin would meet when he was very young.

My father's parents farmed cotton, part of the legacy left by their parents. And that legacy too involved this land. According to records and anecdotes gathered by various genealogists, John Christopher Calvin (1839-1911) from Kentucky married Sara Elizabeth Chaffee from Missouri, the two making their way to Texas shortly after the Civil War. Though they settled first on rural land up around today's Denton, they decided after a while to move further west. In a flourish that makes him seem as detail-oriented as my father the engineer, John listed what he was looking for: a home site with plenty of available water and wood.

He found those things in the Markley community in the northeast corner of Young County, two-hundred and fifty-four acres with enough stone to build a solid house, enough oak to build a rail fence and other buildings, and enough water to keep a spring flowing most of the year. Though the spring supplied enough water for thirteen families, John quickly decided the effort of collecting and delivering it in barrels by wagon was too much of a chore. He let a friend locate a well by "witching" with a forked peach tree limb. Before long, clean, sweet water could be accessed a mere twenty feet underground near the house.

Surely my favorite story about J.C. Calvin centered on the house he built. J.C., I'm thinking, was that type of Texas character who's never satisfied anywhere for long, who's always interested in the next thing for himself and his family. So J.C. had circulars printed up describing the property he was trying to sell in Markley, concentrating most on finding a new place to live. One day, as the family story goes, J.C. picked up a flyer somewhere in his search, read about the good grassland, the generous supply of timber and the water from both spring and well. "There we go," he exclaimed. "I'll buy that!" J.C.'s excitement lasted approximately as long as it took him to realize it was *his* flyer. After that, he was content to live on this land for the remainder of his life.

My great-grandfather and great-grandmother had six children, though one son named Joseph died in his early teens. The others were Robert John (known as Bert), my grandfather (1872-1929); Columbus Charles (known as Lum) (1876-1963); Susan Elizabeth (1881-1944); Arthur Beal (1879-1939); and Thomas Oscar, called Tom (my father's Uncle Tom, who has a big role to play early on) (1883-1957). In one colorful flourish, though perhaps more commonplace on the frontier than in modern times, Bert and Tom married twin sisters, Bert taking Lillie Cooley (1878-1951) as his wife and my grandmother, Tom taking her sister

Wilda (1878-1972). As my grandfather died at a mere fifty-seven and my grandmother lived to be seventy-three, that meant my father and especially his daughter, me, had "Lillie" as part of our lives for a fairly long time.

According to the memories of many connected to Markley, whether they still live nearby or have migrated over the generations to Dallas and environs, the Plum Grove Baptist Church was a center of life, both spiritually and socially. As one Sunday School teacher expressed it back in the early days, "There was nothing really too unusual about my being the teacher—except for the fact that I was then, and always have been, an ardent working Methodist." Plum Grove was an ecumenical kind of place, apparently.

It was also the kind of place, according to one of my family's most enduring stories about Lillie, where people with little money to spare didn't mind working and working and working for the church. Around 1917, even amidst the hardships brought on by America's entry into what was called The Great War, church members decided it was time for a real building to worship in. All kinds of donations were accepted, a $100 gift here, a fifty dollar gift there, even one lady who found a five dollar bill on the road and decided God must have wanted it for the building fund.

Still, nothing produced enough money to get started until my grandmother came up with the idea of the ladies of Plum Grove making a quilt. There would be twenty blocks, and for ten cents a family could have its name embroidered into a square. Everybody remembers Lillie driving her one-horse buggy all over the countryside to sell those squares, visiting the nearby towns and non-towns of Antelope, Jermyn, Loving and Farmer. The Loving Bank, named after Oliver Loving of the Goodnight-Loving cattle trail fame, kicked in five dollars. Or so the story goes. And Lillie even ran out of the house once, using her white cooking apron to wave at a small plane as it flew overheard. "If he'd just land," she declared to her family, "I'd sell him a quilt chance." By all accounts, sadly, the pilot kept on flying.

Once this fundraising technique had raised sixty dollars, the ladies decided to sell chances on who would get to keep the quilt, these being priced at fifty cents each. By the day of the drawing, the ladies of Plum Grove announced proudly they'd raised $120 for the building fund. Lo and behold, the winner of the drawing was...my grandmother. As my father remembered the story, his parents felt the quilt belonged with the pastor in the church that was built, where it stayed for several years. After that, it passed through the hands of various church members until it came back to my father in the mid-1980s.

"I now have the quilt, which has about 650 names, made in 1918 by the ladies of the church," my father wrote to the pastor at the time. "Although the quilt has no intrinsic value, it does have a great deal of sentimental value to me and many others." At some point after that, the quilt ended up at the Young County Museum in the old Post Office in Graham. Word is they display it for the public from time to time. I imagine nobody looking at it today understands how much it has meant to so many.

Another legacy of this period in family history is that I know how to quilt, along with knitting and baking. My grandmother taught me those skills whenever I would spend time with her during summers growing up.

By the time my father was old enough to start school, there was the old schoolhouse in Markley, so that's where he went for his earliest lessons. Considering that he built an impressive academic career later, somebody teaching at the schoolhouse must have been doing something right.

Years later, my father specifically remembered 1909 as the year his future came calling—though, like most of us, he didn't quite recognize it at the time. One day Daddy and his cousin Lillie Mae were walking home from Markley School when they heard the disturbing *toot-toot* of a croaky horn sound directly behind them on the road.

"Elmer, what's *that*?" Lillie Mae asked excitedly.

"Don't be afraid," my father tried to comfort. "That is an *auto-mo-bile*. I saw it in Markley last week."

Lillie Mae was afraid all the same. She crawled under the fence running along that road and ripped a gaping hole in her red and white coat. The driver turned out to be a man named Wilcox who was looking for R. J. Calvin's farm. Elmer let on that

→ *Bear Mountain, Brushy Creek Ranch*

"Bert" was indeed his father and the farm was where he lived, so Mr. Wilcox offered both kids a ride home. My father always took pleasure in this memory of his very first ride in an automobile, not least because he'd spend his entire career building roads and bridges for later generations of cars and trucks.

High school loomed eventually. It's my guess nobody around Markley was thinking much about college. There was talk, I gather, of Bert and Lillie moving the family into Graham, but the costs of doing that proved prohibitive. For a time, it seemed, my father would simply go to work growing cotton on the family land, and that would be his life. My grandmother would hear nothing of it.

"Oh Lord, thanks to my dear mother," my father told me in his final years. "She was so determined that I receive an education that she arranged for me to get room and board with Uncle Tom and Aunt Wilda in Graham, for which I milked and fed their milk cow. And I worked in Uncle Tom's shop each afternoon and Saturdays through my high school days." Tom and Wilda Calvin had two daughters of their own, and over an interlocking series of years they had as many as six teenagers living with them to attend school. Daddy did recall his mother coming to help him with homework many nights.

My father started high school only a year before some of Young County's young men headed off to Europe to fight against Germany in World War I; yet around the town of Graham, most eyes were still focused on a different war that was slowly receding into the past. That very year, the town's white-marble Confederate Infantry memorial was dedicated near the two-story brown sandstone courthouse. That structure, made of stone quarried locally by Irish workers, and that memorial were surely a part of young Elmer's daily life, almost as much as what one contemporary account described as Graham's "magnificent $40,000 high school." In the company of whichever kids were enrolled from Uncle Tom's and Aunt Wilda's, my father walked the half mile to school each morning and home each afternoon.

The town was wildly proud of its high school, which leaders claimed was "without a peer in this section of Texas." Bragging points included the New Oxford individual desks, the "excellent" teachers' desks and chairs, the windows with shades on the inside and heavy screens on the outside, the doors that all opened outward in case of fire and the heat provided in winter by steam. Much was made of the school's water fountains for drinking on hot days, as well as its protection behind "the best iron fence to be found on the market." Most of the teachers had some college or university training plus at least three years of classroom experience. All in all, to the fathers of Graham, the high school Daddy and his cousins attended was one of the finest real estate attractions imaginable.

"Anyone desiring to live in a wide awake town," announced one promotional piece, "where the motto of the school is well equipped buildings, specially trained teachers, and thoroughly educated boys and girls, will do well to come to Graham, buy one or more of the beautiful lots in the new addition near the school buildings, build good homes, and enjoy seeing their children grow up under the most favorable conditions in one of the most progressive school towns in Texas."

Lillie Calvin wanted nothing more, and indeed would accept nothing less, than that very promise for her sons. My father graduated from Graham High School as salutatorian in 1920.

If you wanted to take a sightseeing tour of my father's early life in Young County, you might need a little help from my cousin Tom Loftin, who returned there to live as a rancher and real estate broker after three decades in Texas education; but it could be done. For one thing, three of the most important stops fall within what couldn't be more than one city block.

The old Markley schoolhouse was added onto once or twice since its first students entered in 1891 and before it shut down in 1950, but if you get inside and use your imagination, you can tell where the original building began and ended. These days it's used more as a community center, on those rare occasions when it's used at all. Across the dirt road curving in from Highway 16, there's nothing but open space with a stone marker in the deep-red dirt. All it says is PLUM GROVE BAPTIST CHURCH 1888-1987. The building is gone from here, though you can visit it elsewhere, along another stretch of lonely country highway. As you move deeper onto the property, you reach the main thing you've been searching for.

MARKLEY CEMETERY, the white metal sign reads against the blue sky above the gate, and once you unlatch the chain the gate swings open and you can walk in. Angling to the right, past one historical sign about the Indian Exodus (from Young County to Oklahoma) in the 1850s and another about the Confederate veterans buried here, you reach the section devoted to the Calvins. My great-grandfather J.C. lies here beside the wife he brought to Young County, thus weaving our family's history into the tapestry that is Texas. And there is my grandfather Bert, lying beside his wife Lillie—my father's parents, along with "Little Joe" who died at thirteen, plus two more children who died in infancy.

Directly across Highway 16, you can visit the "old home place" my father grew up on. The spread is padlocked now, used mostly for cattle and hunting. But if you can get inside with help from Cousin Tom, you'll find virtually nothing of the original family cabin—just a rotting rendition of an outhouse. You can also drive along the edges of J.C.'s original spread, the one he tried to sell until he fell in love with it all over again, standing at the modern fence and gazing across at the open green fields, seeing again why this land had treated him so well.

In Graham itself, you can swing around the edge of Shawnee Park and follow directions a couple more blocks to Brazos Street. There, at number 810, you find a charming white house with a deep gallery across the front, chairs set out for any neighbors who drop by. This is (or was, before some modernization) the home of Uncle Tom and Aunt Wilda, who took in my father during his high school years and treated him as one of their own. It seems comfortable, welcoming, unpretentious. It was those things and more for four years of Elmer Calvin's life.

All these years later, it's hard to say exactly how my father settled on the college he would attend or even, beyond my grandmother's encouragements, decided that he would go to college at all. It seemed to have something to do with being there at the center of life in Graham, his Uncle Tom not only running the blacksmith shop and belonging to the town band and volunteer fire unit but also winning a spot on the town council and serving as a deacon in the First Baptist Church. As one local historian put it, "Tom was liked by everyone, and many of the local fellows would visit the shop because they knew he always had a funny story to tell, a smile and a word of cheer."

I can speak to this quality in Uncle Tom, having spent holidays with him and especially having seen it in my father. Looking through his writings after his death, the bulk of my father's words are devoted to anecdotes, vignettes and other things that might make people smile. It's not too much to imagine that he picked up these tendencies, these gifts, working beside Uncle Tom at the blacksmith shop.

It sounds odd today, but my family retains a memory of a certain university sending a truck around the rural areas to recruit promising students. My father was such a promising student, and no doubt they'd heard of him. At least as important, there was a neighboring rancher named Prideaux who offered to help with Daddy's tuition. So the truck came by, my family insists, and my father went away—to the Army-affiliated Corps of Cadets at a university two hundred and fifty-five miles to the southeast: Texas A&M.

ONCE A
Cadet

CHAPTER TWO

By September 16, 1920—the day my
father and his fellow freshmen "reported for
duty" at Texas A&M—the university was
embarking on a period of dramatic change
and expansion. Of course, none of the young
men from across Texas and beyond could have
known that at the time.

With its attachment to military discipline
and tradition passed down through its iconic
Corps of Cadets, the land-grant school had
been delivering instruction in the Brazos
Valley town of College Station since 1876,
with its School of Engineering occupying the
same building since 1909. Yet before my father
could pick up his degree four years later, A&M would struggle
to educate battle-weary survivors of Europe's Great War, endure
two scandals over the hazing of freshmen, construct several new
buildings and add many new academic concentrations. It would
also spotlight one of my father's own engineering classmates in
the school's most enduring athletic legend.

My father never told me about the first day he ventured into
the tan-brick, classically inclined civil engineering building; but
if you visit the sprawling campus today, it hasn't changed much.

→ *Elmer as a young cadet*

You can still enter through the main doors, gazing upward at the four white Ionian columns that serve as facade to floors two and three. You can still climb the switchback central staircase, just as Daddy did for the first time in 1920, and move along the hallways glancing into classrooms and professors' offices.

With a little digging, you can learn that five-hundred and one young men had earned civil engineering degrees before my father's arrival, along with two young women described as twin daughters of an A&M history professor. And you can certainly learn that J.C. Nagle was the legendary department head, with two full professors and several lesser ranks below him. Nagle had first been with A&M from 1890 to 1913, and then returned in 1917. A plaque beside the entrance lets on that students had a habit of calling him "Jimmie," presumably behind his back. Yet above the glass doors is a far more official utterance: Since 1929, the civil engineering building has been called Nagle Hall.

It was, most historians admit, a strange time to enter Texas A&M as a freshman—or, in the dismissive parlance used on campus, a "fish." While the university and its habits must have shown every sign of being timeless, the larger world was changing more rapidly than it had in anyone's memory. Most would blame this change on, or credit this change to, the conflict still being described all-too-optimistically as the "War to End All Wars."

Only months before my father's arrival on campus, in fact, the 1920 yearbook (called the Longhorn, as though oblivious to future confusion with A&M's arch-rival school in Austin) had opened with a photo section paying tribute to the fifty-one students who were killed overseas. The yearbook quoted the *New York Times* as saying A&M had sent more young Americans to fight than any other school its size, more than 2,500 of its "sons" in all. In the inflated language of that era, the fifty-one pictured on these pages had "died so gloriously for the principles in which they believed." The 20th century, contrary to expectation at the time, would provide several more opportunities for yearbook staffs to employ such language.

The end of hostilities in Europe and the coming of the 1920s produced almost numberless traumas. Thanks to Henry Ford, streets once filled with horse-drawn carriages started to fill with noisy horseless ones. And the moral fibers that had long bound small town to small town began to shred under pressure from those who'd gone overseas, where they'd seen simplistic American beliefs about life put to the test and were often found wanting. Soon to be dubbed "The Lost Generation," these newly cynical young people plunged headlong into the Jazz Age, the Roaring Twenties, where women were striving to be "flappers" and men "jellybeans." Without faith in any greater good—how *could* they believe, after the terrors they'd seen—they reverted to a life of pleasure found in driving, drinking, dancing and, of course, sex.

By all accounts, there were no jellybeans, and especially no flappers, on the A&M campus. But there were all those veterans. Perhaps understandably, few groups were more traumatized in the years after World War I.

Until John "Blackjack" Pershing's departure for Europe as head of the Expeditionary Force, most American young people had followed their parents' instructions, their preachers' instructions and, when the time came, their college professors' instructions. Having taken orders to the brink of death, however, veterans who returned to complete their studies bristled at every command. And their professors had no other skills to achieve the desired result. Campus debates broke out over many things, yet no issue so much as the school's mandatory military training. These veterans of the trenches felt they should be excused from drilling ceremoniously up and down *anybody's* parade ground, but the school for a time stuck to its position. Logic won out eventually, and the veterans were given a dispensation.

Not so, of course, for incoming "fish" like my father. By

tradition (already a holy word around A&M, as used often in the Longhorn as well as the campus newspaper, the *Batallion*), freshmen were subjected to hazing from the day of their arrival. Some was mere subservience to upperclassmen, while some constituted true verbal abuse. And finally, there was at least some physical abuse, enough to spark reports of fatalities. As the hazing scandal mounted in 1920 (only to reappear before Daddy's graduation in 1924), a series of hearings was held by the Texas Senate. No hazing deaths could be confirmed, despite the rumors. In the end, legislators voted to outlaw hazing just as my father and his classmates were getting their freshman bags unpacked.

"We were dashed from our castles of immediate success to the life of a lowly 'fish,'" the Class of 1924 reported in a later yearbook, before briefly summarizing the scandal. "The School's reputation was in our hands, and it was only our class spirit and close cooperation with the upper classmen that made an abrupt change easy."

During his freshman year, my father took the same courses as students in any other branch of engineering, such as electrical, mechanical or chemical. Even through sophomore and junior years, he had little room for electives. It was only in his senior year that my father was able to concentrate on civil engineering courses, with specific training related to highways. This area generated particular pride around the building, especially since the state's Highway Engineer (described as "the highest salaried public official in Texas") was a graduate of the program, as was a man working in that capacity for another state. Indeed, A&M engineering could boast graduates working across the United States, as well as in Mexico, Central and South America, India, Korea and other foreign countries. "Everywhere they have given good account of themselves," the school beamed.

Non-academic, non-military "student life" was mentioned

→ *Studying in the dorm*

only briefly in yearbooks and campus papers, much less than it would be in those same media deeper into the 20th century. A more detailed look comes to us from a novel written after my father's departure but long before wholesale changes had occurred on campus and off. The self-published fiction by John O. Pasco, titled *Fish Sergeant*, describes the first year endured by a cadet named Elmer Hook, who predictably becomes known to his presumed betters as "Fish Hook."

The book sketches in many Aggie traditions, including the Elephant Walk by seniors each Thanksgiving Day, Fish Day when freshmen ruled the school and the final presentation of Reserve Officer commissions on the day after commencement. Nothing in the book, however, is more entertaining than its dictionary of A&M slang: "Prexy" for the college president, "sawdust" for sugar, "shotgun" for pepper sauce, "cush" for dessert and "dope" for coffee.

As reflected in the letters home that form *Fish Sergeant*, the closest supply of young women sanctioned by A&M could be found at the Texas State College for Women in Denton. Indeed any account of Aggie life from my father's time into the 1940s had to include tales of hitchhiking north to find a date. On the bright side, it was said that any cadet in an A&M uniform stepping onto the women's campus had a good chance of finding companionship. These romantic adventures took their place among all the others to form what Pasco refers to as Aggie Spirit. "You will never find an Aggie who is not more than glad to tell you of his experience with the spirit," he writes. "It is something that just gets hold of you and you have cold chills, a cold sweat, a fever, a nervous breakdown, and the biggest thrill of your life at the same time."

Elmer Ben Calvin was not one of those adults who talked incessantly of college into his later years. Still, he always expressed admiration and gratitude to College Station for giving him the tools to succeed (and travel the earth) as much as he did.

The final *Battalion* of my father's A&M career, dated May 6, 1924, curiously carries no story about the graduates, commencement or the presentation of commissions. Still, the edition is bookended by two features that grab the eye. One is a front-page letter by beloved university president William Bennett Bizzell (referred to as "Prexy" in the headline) from his travels in Europe. "The net result of it all," he writes to his students from Switzerland, "is to cause one to love his own country more and appreciate more intensely the privilege of living under free institutions."

The back page, to modern eyes, is a truly bizarre ad from Westinghouse Electric that only an engineering student could love. Lengthy text celebrates the victory of what was called "Westinghouse current" after the "bitter struggle...due to its supposedly deadly characteristics." My father, of course, would have understood. The victorious form of electricity is what we know as alternating current, finally rising above the "direct current" championed by no less than Thomas Edison. There is no mention of the Wizard of Menlo Park in the Westinghouse advertisement.

Though my father was never obsessed with football, coming of age before "fun" and "recreation" had replaced constant work as parts of college life, he did forever afterward claim to have helped his alma mater win a football game—without ever going out on the field. According to the tale, he and his engineering buddies were asked to make some improvements to the place where games were played (the site of today's Kyle Field). This they did, preparing for a new playing surface by digging a ditch along one side—in football terms, on the sideline out of bounds. "On Thanksgiving Day 1923," Daddy recalled, "A&M and Texas were tied 0-0 at the half. On the first play after the third-quarter kickoff, the Aggies' left end hid in the ditch I had dug, only to jump up, run onto the playing field unnoticed and catch a touchdown pass." This was a very interesting play, I think.

As the cadets gathered for their big day, another young man my father studied beside was already taking on the makings of mythology. That student had played football for A&M—had, in fact, lettered eight times in football, basketball and baseball—and had been there in Dallas on January 2, 1922, for the "miraculous" Aggie victory over the Centre College Praying Colonels in the Dixie Classic, an early version of the Cotton Bowl. The engineering student had not suited out for that game, but was watching from the stands. When, however, A&M's coach (colorfully named D.X. Bible) noticed his squad shrinking from injury after injury, he called the student down and had him change into an injured player's uniform.

The student never played a single down that day, but many decided his presence gave the team the confidence it needed to win. After graduation, he went on to Baylor College of Medicine and served as a doctor for four decades in Corpus Christi.

He retired to Rockport before passing away at age seventy-four in December 1976. Today there's a statue of Dr. E. King Gill, in that borrowed uniform, in front of Kyle Field. Most fans of Aggie elevens across the ages know him simply as "The Twelfth Man".

My father's face gazes up at me from the 1924 Longhorn, one of four faces on each of the sixty-two pages. He looks youthful and handsome, serious but with a twinkle that seems like playfulness in his eyes. I learn that his college nicknames were E.B. and Major, and that his most notable affiliations were the Pistol Team and the Pistol Club. Daddy was never an elected class officer, but I don't think the father I knew would have bothered to campaign. Most of all, looking down at the page in the reading room of A&M's Cushing Library, I am touched by what some unidentified classmate wrote about him, using the clever, tongue-in-cheek style favored in all such passages.

> "Elmer is one of the most promising disciples of the Cue Ball," I read. "If ambition, determination and good judgment will bring success, his fortune is assured. His present ambition is to revolutionize railroad building in South America. He is a true friend and a loyal son of A&M. We expect great things from you, Elmer."

Those five sentences penned about my father at the close of his years in College Station are wonderfully affectionate, I believe. And more than a little prophetic.

→ *Elmer at pistol practice*

YOUNG
Engineer

CHAPTER THREE

I of course can't know if my father got his first job with the Texas Highway Department because its chief engineer was from A&M—but it couldn't have hurt. The older man had sat in the same desks my father had so recently vacated, taken many of the same courses, feared or fought or tried to charm the same professors, probably even J.C. Nagle himself. The chief engineer knew how *much* my father knew, even that he'd been able to take those highway electives near the end, so it made sense to want him on the team. Still, what my father thought he had in store joining the department in 1924 was a

→ *Starting out as an engineer*

far cry from what he had to look back on when the gathering clouds of history carried him away to the U.S. Army eighteen years later.

There was always plenty of work to be done, dragging Texas out of its dusty or muddy past left over from the state's beginnings in the mid-19th century. Still, few in the department or out of it could have guessed that highway construction in Texas was about to enter a mostly unplanned golden age. Really, how many lines of work can say *that* about the Great Depression?

Arriving at the Highway Department in the summer of 1924, my father had a more-than-adequate mastery of general engineering, from initial design to final completion. But within a few months, his special interest had made itself plain: contractors and the contracts that established the conditions of their work. Operating in a still-new arena where government control interacted with countless private companies, this expertise would prove crucial. Like his eventual mentor, General Leslie Groves of the Manhattan Project, my father would become a walking encyclopedia of who did what and how much they charged for it in construction. It was the industrial equivalent of the traditional rural housewife, who knew where in the open-air market to buy everything from chickens to potatoes, and not get charged too much for them. Guys like General Groves and my father didn't just show up on a new assignment with their knowledge; they showed up with what a later generation would call their Rolodex.

→ *Tough work in Texas*

Operating at the still-new intersection of government funding and private execution, my father had to learn quickly, and mostly by doing, how to be both good cop and bad cop—especially when dealing with contractors who might cut corners in ways that were unacceptable, or even dangerous. And he had to master the twin dynamics of any construction job, budget and deadline. In his early years with the Texas Highway Department, budget tended to be king, with all the approvals and spending authorizations in place. Years later, in a dramatic switch, the Manhattan Project would give my father a budget so open-ended as to be nearly non-existent. The deadline, on the other hand, would rule. The world had no idea that top-secret construction was under way in Oak Ridge, Hanford and Los Alamos, but it was waiting.

From 1924 until 1929, in his first job out of Texas A&M, my father served the Texas Highway Department as Location Engineer and Assistant Resident Engineer for Shackelford and Throckmorton counties, wild and wooly areas around dramatic Palo Duro Canyon that still considered themselves part of the Old West. To this day, locals take newcomers to visit Fort Griffith on a clear fork of the Brazos, seeming especially proud of the area outside the fort known as The Flat or Hide Town, a cluster of ruined buildings that once served up gambling, alcohol and loose women to lawmen like Pat Garrett, Doc Holliday and Wyatt Earp, as well as to outlaws like John Wesley Hardin. Highway design, as opposed to local lore, was my father's world each day as he headed out from Albany, from route studies to location surveys, contractor estimates to construction supervision. He must have done an excellent job, for in 1929 my father was transferred to the state capital at Austin, spending the next dozen years handling similar assignments in one or two surrounding counties.

While it's certainly not true that the road system my father took on during these years was unchanged since the Texas Republic, it did carry elements—including poor quality and limited coverage—that had plagued the state from its start. Indeed, little had changed foundationally about Texas roads, and especially their routes, since the days of ancient Indian trails. The Spanish had followed the native trails, and many contemporary routes continued on the same paths.

The roads they took over with most vigor were those that linked key points of their empire, which was known then as New Spain but eventually as Mexico. The central government in Mexico City needed access to its far-flung holdings in places like San Antonio and Goliad, and to the even more remote missions in today's East Texas. That meant roads, more like paths really, like the Old San Antonio, the La Bahia and, in the east, Trammel's Trace. You can see marked-out remnants of the Old San Antonio, for instance, when you visit Fort Davis in West Texas, and it's not very impressive: two side-by-side paths as far apart as wagon ruts, with grass growing around all the edges.

After the bloodshed of the Texas Revolution—the Alamo, of course, and the Texas victory at San Jacinto near today's Houston—there was a plan by the Republic to construct a Central National Road to help attract fresh settlers. With statehood and its new organization, however, came a wider commitment to clear forty-foot-wide paths between all county seats. These were optimistically known as "first-class roads," not to be confused with "second-class roads" that were thirty feet wide and "third-class roads" that were only twenty-two.

With a constitutional amendment in 1883, the state assumed power to tax residents to fund county roads. Virtually all early roads in Texas were built by the counties, with commissioners deciding which petitions from landowners would be accepted and which would be rejected. This was immense power, considering the circumstances of survival in rural areas, and it made for virtually unavoidable graft and the inefficiencies that flow in every direction from it.

Interestingly, the labor to do the actual work (even into the 20th century) was drawn from local landowners. By Texas law, all able-bodied men between the ages of eighteen and forty-five had to "volunteer" several days a year to work under county overseers. As some landowners accrued resources through farming, cattle ranching or other occupations, it became common for these to hire surrogates—thus producing the first *paying* highway jobs in Texas.

From an engineering perspective, the thinking behind the earliest Texas roads (when we can see thinking at all) was quite different from the ideas taught to my father by his A&M professors. Early roads, for one thing, didn't always connect to any larger web the way we have today. They tended to begin and

→ *Early Texas highways*

end, as reflected in names like the Blanco-San Antonio Road. For another thing, since early builders had no technology to remove hills, boulders or even larger trees, the roads simply went around them—creating wild zigzag patterns along the route, right-angle turns and spot after spot that couldn't drain away rainwater. The roads, therefore, were almost impassable with dust, except when they were almost impassable with mud. And while the lack of a hard surface was par for the course in much of America, the end result was slow going indeed.

In more ways than Texas can count, everything changed with the automobile.

Drivers were the first to notice—how could they not be—that roads that once satisfied people on foot or in wagons were utterly impractical for cars. In one famous social development, "Good Roads" organizations grew up around the state, promoting auto tours and organizing volunteer days of highway cleaning and improvement. Many in Texas saw a need for some form of highway department as early as 1903, but nothing was done until 1916, when the federal government mandated that each state have such a thing. That first year, no fewer than 194,720 autos were registered in the state, a tiny number compared to now but surely more than we might expect. The department's job was to grant financial aid to counties so they could build and maintain "their" roads, a job that got easier in 1921 when the federal government agreed to match every dollar. There was, we can see, a growing consensus that Americans needed to get around and that only better roads would allow them to do so.

In 1924, the year of my father's graduation, the state took on the responsibility of maintaining all state highways. By the next year, it had solidified its authority to construct a state highway "system" in lieu of just putting a road here and another road there at the behest of county commissioners. Texas developed its first statewide markings during my father's first years on the job, setting out signs with mileage and directions on both state and federal highways. It was a huge job to accomplish that alone, yet the job of actually creating the highways those signs would mark was even more so.

Like every other state in the union, Texas suffered mightily when the Depression took hold in late 1929 and, within two or three years, ground whatever had passed for an economy to a halt. Texas was primarily a rural state—not just with "miles and miles" of open space but with a population that depended on small-scale farming, just as my father's family had in Markley. As the Depression kicked the chair out from under such dealings, more and more rural families in Texas and the rest of America's heartland headed for the big cities to look for work. Before long, that meant the big cities were overwhelmed as much as the countryside.

Looking back, one of the few specific groups spared by the Depression were highway engineers like Elmer Calvin. Within a decade, funds flowing into their efforts (in Texas via Congressman John Nance Garner, later to serve as Franklin Roosevelt's New Deal vice president) didn't merely allow highway engineers to continue feeding their families. They allowed these engineers to connect

→ *Bridge over troubled water*

parts of the state that had never been connected, paving the way (in some cases literally) for commerce that would encourage the state's and nation's recovery. In light of my father's full career, we also can't overlook the fact that improved, expanded highways made for a military that could better respond to threats from countries that still seemed very far away.

When people think of the Works Progress Administration and other New Deal construction programs like the Civilian Conservation Corps, it's easy to think their primary purpose was to create jobs for starving Americans. Arguably that was their primary purpose, especially in the way the jobs were parceled out to one "breadwinner" per family. The idea was to keep the nation afloat until recovery kicked in, not merely to get a project finished. Still, if you don't think important things got done during that period, just drive around Texas.

Many remote bridges over rivers, creeks, canyons and ravines still carry construction dates carved in them from that period, and a lot of the highways connecting those bridges to each other hail from the same era. In addition, the state is filled today with historic constructions, from tourist camps and visitor facilities to dams that turned rivers into lakes to produce electricity—all functions of the WPA, and therefore also functions of the Texas Highway Department.

There was a political element to all this dazzling progress in Texas at a time so many states were making little or none. At the ideological level, many engineers had deep thoughts about what better (and better landscaped) highways might mean: they would usher society from the past toward the future. To this day, drivers through Texas are struck by the many cultural and historical references to Old Texas—longhorns, wagons, cowboys, flora and fauna—that find their way into highway and roadside designs. This was purposeful, reminding Texans of their uniqueness as a people and pointing them toward a cleaner, brighter, faster, more productive future that waited at the far end of the road. Obviously, Texans must not have considered themselves included when humorist Will Rogers called America the "only nation that ever drove to the poorhouse in an automobile." In the Lone Star State, the automobile and the fuel it ran on were things that kept you *out* of the poorhouse.

→ *Building an overpass, 1930s*

In addition to ideology, there was that other kind of Texas politics, the kind that at the height of the Depression relied on cheerleading slogans like, "Get the Farmer out of the Mud." Roads became a huge deal in Texas, as nothing seemed to inspire confidence and improve living conditions quicker than being connected to someplace else. With the federal funding local politicians could boast about bringing to their towns, districts and state, Texas built more "Good Roads" than the earlier movement's believers even dreamed of.

Much effort and investment went into major trunk roads between Texas cities and the state's more important towns, but the highway work that transformed the landscape most was what still goes by the letters FM: Farm-to-Market roads, an entire system running past "the farmer's front door," as an early champion put it. These were essential to progress within the state, engineers of my father's day understood. They would make making a living a little easier (though nothing could ever make farming easy), along with ushering in electric power lines, faster mail delivery, better consolidated schools, and improved access to medical care. As many relics from the past attest, these roads also opened the eyes of Texas to quirky early notions of tourism.

Attractions built around bits of local history or scenery, plus the usual odd array of Indian artifacts and rattlesnakes, cropped up all over Texas, waiting for the next car to pull off the new road onto the gravel parking lot. Along with these came a series of roadside parks, constructed by local volunteer groups with additional labor provided by the National Youth Administration. Texas women in particular rallied around these rest stops, working to limit the billboard advertising that, then as now, would spoil all the great views. The Texas Highway Department created the Office of Landscape Architect in 1933, ostensibly to plan beautification for the state's centennial three years later but also given the twin, ongoing mandates of aesthetics and driving safety.

There was one additional motivation and urgency to Texas highway work at this time. The same drought that produced the Dust Bowl in Oklahoma, creating the "Okies" and other desperate souls captured in John Steinbeck's novel *The Grapes of Wrath* (and of course, by Henry Fonda in the classic movie), was tearing into the heart of Texas. Erosion in the "dirty thirties," a period of droughts, dust storms and floods, became a fear verging on national hysteria. "Calm down," the Texas highway engineers seemed to say at public hearing after public hearing: Erosion may be "the great highway destroyer," but new and better highways built on new and better science could actually *prevent* erosion. New highways, when generously surrounded by native plants, held the soil together at the same time they were holding the people together.

Yes, you can look up statistics as well as I can. But since my father came of age as an engineer during this effort, I decided it was worth finding some scope and scale. Between 1935 and 1943, in Texas alone, the WPA/THD partnership constructed 31,836 miles of new and improved roads; 7,686 new and improved bridges; and 34,431 new culverts. The $159.6 million spent on highway construction represented almost forty percent of the WPA's total spending—an impressive proportion, I'd say—and naturally it also did what it initially set out to do: put people to work. It's not for nothing that workers of that day carved the name and year of each job into the concrete monuments they left behind. At a time of confusion, bitterness and shame, those guys were proud of what they'd done.

In the process, even as the WPA was embraced by many as their savior, the real importance of the Texas Highway Department expanded rather than contracted. The bulk of the work's funding came from the federal level, but the THD was never shy about deciding how to spend it. And the system worked, at least for and in Texas. As early in the Depression as 1932, the state took on the burden of paying highway debts generated by the counties, which were all broke or dangerously close to it. In 1937, the THD took over construction and maintenance in all towns with fewer than 2,500 residents, as well as in cities whose houses were more than 200 feet apart.

→ *Gibb Gilchrist, Texas highway director*

Contrary to what we'd presume today, the THD didn't merely carry out the wishes of what we picture as federal bureaucrats in Washington. It was those federal bureaucrats who ended up funding the wishes of engineers here in Texas. It was the THD, with engineers like Elmer Calvin, who received proposals for work from WPA districts all over the state, and then sent the list of projects *it* chose to Washington for blanket approval. By all accounts, this was a system created by Texas road engineers *for* Texas road engineers, who felt they knew the best ways to connect the distant corners of the state anyway. "Any other policy," warned the legendary Gibb Gilchrist, my father's top boss at the time, "must result in chaos."

Beginning during our Austin years, and continuing off and on for the rest of his life, my father developed a habit of jotting down things that made him smile and/or think: clever vignettes, witty phrases, entertaining visuals, mini-stories with a twist at the end that would remind many of O. Henry. That, apparently, was the kind of writing in my father's personal water supply. Sometimes, perusing these tales today, I want to beg him for more information about the one thing he seemingly most took for granted: his work building roads and bridges across Texas. But they are what he chose to write down, what he chose to leave for those of us who came after him. The earliest I have is a two-pager he titled "Another Fitting Moment," which began in 1936 when he was resident engineer building a steel arch bridge over the Colorado River at Marble Falls.

→ *Bridge below Buchanan Dam*

During that job, my father tells of visiting one Mr. Darragh, who operated the red-granite mountain works, and admiring (as a lifelong rock enthusiast and collector) a slab of granite leaning against the corner of the man's office. "Would you like a piece of that?" Darragh asked. "It is opaline granite. At this time there are only two known deposits—one in Llano, Texas, and one in Bavaria, Germany. It is hard; it is un-economical to use in buildings. It is used sometimes for small items, such as monuments." Though it took considerable effort to liberate a small piece, my father had opaline granite with him that day by the time he left Darragh's office.

My father switches narrative gears at this point in his story, telling of his interest in Wilbarger County just west of Wichita Falls and its namesake, Josiah Pugh Wilbarger. One day Wilbarger and a friend were out hiking near Bastrop in the Lost Pines area east of Austin when they were set upon by Comanches. The Indians scalped the men and left them for dead, but Wilbarger did not die. He was nursed back to health by his family and lived eleven more years, dying a natural death. "Lord," my father admits some might be tempted to say, "He had a hard head." But Daddy thought that a harsh thing to say about a patriot of the Texas Revolution, preferring to say Wilburger "had a strong constitution."

As my father relates, he went for a drive in the country in 1938 and noticed an old cemetery with a wire fence around it. He admits being unable to resist the temptation to read the grave markers, so he pulled the car to the side of the road. He read in an excited voice from one of the gravestones. "Josiah Pugh Wilbarger, 1801-1845, A Patriot of the Texas Republic." Even better, the monument was made of opaline granite, reminding him of his conversation with Mr. Darragh. "What a fitting monument," he remembered thinking.

In so many ways, at least one that would prove important to my father's postwar career, the same kinds of issues my father dealt with in the 1920s and 1930s were being discussed on the regional and national level as they were in Texas. As it turns out, there had been something known as the American Road & Transportation Builders Associations (ARTBA) since the early 1920s. Though it played a few different roles over the decades, one of its most important was keeping the federal government involved in highways even after its initial effort had been declared a big failure.

⇢ *Checking out the new bridge*

In 1916, the Federal Aid-Road Act outlined a partnership with each state intended to facilitate the construction of highways in response to increasing numbers of personal autos, the birth of the modern trucking industry at the expense of rail and the beginnings of America's first massive consumer economy. Sadly, much of this effort foundered, especially during the trauma of World War I. After investors and even amateur contractors had attempted to follow the federal money, prices shot up among all buildings materials but especially those siphoned for the war effort. Road building wages shot up too, with the effect that many projects went bankrupt, and a wartime shortage of railroad cars meant that even the highway's natural nemesis couldn't step into the breach. Loud voices demanded the dismantling of the entire partnership, until the first fulltime paid executive of the ARTBA spoke up.

"The heavy truck...has shown that it has solved an economic problem," the executive argued in 1918, the year he became the organization's director. He disagreed with many highway executives who felt that trucking would always be only a short-haul affair. "The heavy truck will be utilized in transporting freight and express within expanding limits. We must build and maintain in such a way that our roads will withstand, as permanently as possible, the demands of the future heavy truck traffic."

That ARTBA director, also sometimes referred to as "The Father of the Modern Highway," was Charles M. Upham. In Elmer Calvin's life, long after many problems with the federal-state partnership had been ironed out by the Highway Act of 1921, Upham would turn up again.

→ *Connecting Texas with roads and bridges*

WINDS
of War

CHAPTER FOUR

Happily for my father, he didn't have
to follow the depressing news from Europe
and Asia alone, whether it came via headlines
in the daily newspapers or over the radios
around which Americans gathered anxiously
each night. Beginning in Albany and
throughout his years in Austin, a woman was
by his side. Before the move from one Texas
town to the other, Agnes Standlee became
Elmer Calvin's wife. Agnes, of course, was
my mother.

➤ *Elmer and Agnes as young couple*

Different strands of the Standlee family
arrived, as Standlee, Standilee and Standley,
just to make the genealogical research challenging. In the case
of my mother, she was born in Cornelius, Oregon on April 28,
1898, making her almost four years older than my father. Her
parents are listed as "Dr. and Mrs." Claud Standlee, thus setting
the stage for an affinity for education that would guide both her
life and that of her brother Earle. It certainly guided her life once
the family moved to an area of Texas between Young County,
where my father would grow to manhood, and Shackleford
County, where my parents would meet and begin sixty-eight
years of marriage.

Growing up in Texas, with my mother's earliest life filtered through her many years here, we didn't know very much about her time in Oregon. Still, a little bit of checking has turned up more than a little bit of interest.

Yes, my grandfather Claud was a doctor in Oregon, mainly treating (as family oral history asserts) Native Americans. And that ties in with his residence in Drewsey, a small town where Oregon's Paiute Indians camped on the banks of the Malheur River. Within his lifetime, the area was designated the Malheur Indian Reservation for "all the roving and straggling bands of eastern and southeastern Oregon, which can be induced to settle there." In those days, having a doctor to treat your many illnesses was probably inducement indeed, as was financial and other aid from the government to encourage farming rather than "roving and straggling." Many Paiutes took the government up on its offer, settling along the river, which, in those days before dams and other changes in the waterway, also had abundant salmon for fishing.

All the same, Dr. Claud Standlee wasn't merely the local MD, another of Drewsey's official population of eighteen—a number that clearly didn't include anyone living on the reservation. He was, according to a story tucked into the long gray columns of the *Sunday Oregonian* published in Portland on August 26, 1900, the town's mayor.

By the time of the article headlined "Prosperity in Drewsey: Thriving Harney County Town Livestock and Lumber Interests," however, our family's vision of Dr. Claud taking care of the "poor Indians" had apparently become a memory. During what's known locally as the Bannock Indian War of 1878, the Paiutes he cared for scattered across reservations in Idaho, Nevada and California, leaving behind twelve thousand tillable acres for incoming whites who started claiming "squatter's rights" almost before the former residents' campfires burned down. This produced rapid growth and even a modicum of civic pride. "The Town of Drewsey," offers one local history, a tad cryptically, "has a wide reputation for its energy and life a long distance away. Drewsey has been quiet this summer, but it is picking up now." Evidence of this includes several new residences under construction, an Odd Fellows hall expected to cost $2,000 and a "good school" where two teachers taught seventy-five pupils. The town, in fact, had only recently been incorporated, with my grandfather as its first mayor.

→ *Agnes in early years of marriage*

Undeniably, a major event in my mother's youth was her father's early death. Claud was only thirty-nine when he passed away in Erath County, Texas, where his grave still resides. How and why he moved the family to Texas between 1900 and his death in 1908 remains something of a mystery, addressed only by a bit of our family's lore.

Whatever the timeline might be, we were brought up believing Dr. Claud contracted tuberculosis (or consumption, as it was usually called in those days) during his years working among the Indians. This is possible, however many years most Paiutes had been gone from this piece of the Pacific Northwest—just as it is logical a terminally ill Claud moved his family to Texas in pursuit of a drier, healthier climate, as many people did at the time. Or perhaps, since both Claud and his wife Beatrice were originally from Arkansas, he simply wanted to be closer to home and family when he died. They settled in tiny Huckabay initially, but later moved to the Erath county seat called Stephenville ten miles to the southeast. Beatrice Standlee lived to be seventy-one, passing away in 1943 having, by all accounts written or remembered, never remarried.

→ *Swimming at El Rancho Rio*

With seeming ease, my mother studied at John Tarleton College in Stephenville and finally the College of Industrial Arts in Denton (today's Texas Woman's University). After her marriage to my father and their move to Austin in 1929, she completed her bachelor's degree at University of Texas and, later still, her master's at the San Marcos College of Arts, now Texas State University. Apparently, one's master's thesis, like charity, begins close to home: Agnes wrote hers on the beautification movement focused on Texas highways.

In between those stints as a student, Agnes was a teacher—first in Kerrville in the Hill Country and finally in Albany. In all, she'd work as a teacher for twenty-six years, in several Texas school districts, as well as traveling with my father on business in South America, Africa and Asia. "Her teaching philosophy was grounded," we wrote in her 1994 obituary, "in solid foundations of reading, writing and phonics at an elementary level. To her students she provided daily inspiration grounded in strong moral values." I couldn't describe Agnes Standlee Calvin any better or any differently all these years after her death, as a teacher, as a wife or as my mother.

As it turns out, Agnes wasn't the only half of this couple pursuing education. Early on in Austin, my father heard about a night

→ *Carolyn riding Chiquita*

class in law. While the course was intended for students planning to take the bar exam and then actually practice law (two things Daddy had no intention of doing), he did see considerable value to his work as an engineer at the Texas Highway Department in mastering the basic concepts. He signed up for classes in contract law—a registration that in some ways would change his life—as well as in "riparian rights," governing landowners along rivers.

Also during the pre-war period, my parents' lives grew more serious, what today we'd probably call more "grounded." For one thing, in Austin, they were able to purchase their first house, a cute brick residence on 32nd Street and Waller Creek less than a mile from the UT athletic field. But, as my father expressed it in retrospect, his acquisitiveness wasn't satisfied by a single residence. "I always wanted to own some land," he wrote, "and one day, with a little cash and a big vendor's lien note, I bought a 1,300-acre tract along the Colorado River about three-quarter miles and extending south to a small country road for the entrance. We named it El Rancho Rio."

All this expansion happened around the same time our family was expanding. I entered the picture on September 16, 1941. My parents were thrilled, as they were getting older and, especially in those days, couples their age feared they couldn't or wouldn't have children at all.

I'm thinking that my two earliest memories occurred at the ranch rather than at our house near the university. In the first, I woke up from a nap screaming and crying because I realized there was nobody racing in to check on me. I remember standing at the window holding my Raggedy Ann doll and waiting for someone—anyone—to come make me feel safe. From my grown-up perspective, I now imagine my parents had stepped outside and locked the door, probably to keep me from wandering off.

My second memory must have happened a year or two later. My father had a black stallion by the name of Ranger (never to be confused with the sweet little paint pony he'd bought me to ride, Chiquita), and one day he took me with him to bird hunt on a cliff above the river. "Hold the reins," he told me, getting ready to shoot. "And do not let go!" Well, my father's shotgun made its usual ear-shaking roar, and Ranger bolted up onto his hind legs, yanking the reins right out of my hands and running away. My father was furious, even though he was relieved Ranger's hooves hadn't come down on me. I'm sure I screamed or cried, or both. It must have been a long walk home to the ranch house. And Ranger must have been really mean, since a neighboring rancher eventually shot him.

If my father's timing in life and career was typically uncanny, *my* timing now strikes me as less so. Not even three months after I was born, my father took my mother and me on a motorboat ride down the river from the ranch toward Austin, only to return to find his gathered workers upset about news coming in from Hawaii. It was December 7th. The Japanese were attacking our base at a place called Pearl Harbor.

Just as a future generation would ask "Where were you when JFK was shot in Dallas?" my parents' contemporaries would spend the rest of their lives asking each other, "Where were you when you heard about Pearl Harbor?" The

→ *Elmer and Agnes show off Carolyn*

assault on American soil, not equaled in trauma until the terrorists attacks of 9/11 aimed at New York and Washington, marked and indeed defined a generation of Americans. Already, referring to the Great Depression, President Roosevelt had promised them a "rendezvous with destiny." How well they survived that first horror and then World War II would earn them another nickname. My parents, typical of their time, place and attitude, surely never

→ *The young Army officer*

thought of theirs as "The Greatest Generation." They merely figured they, as Americans, had a job to do.

Pearl Harbor changed everything. "What a depressing feeling!" my father would write about that December 7th, but for him and millions of others in this country, the feeling quickly gave way to quiet anger and finally, commitment. As Daddy remembered it, "the next day or so" he talked with his bosses at the Highway Department, and they agreed he should volunteer for active duty with the U.S. Army Corps of Engineers. And a friend who had already done so told the commanders at Fort Sam Houston in San Antonio about his mastery of contracts. With the amount of infrastructure required for improving existing military facilities like Sam Houston and building new ones from the ground up like Camp Hood (now Fort Hood), there would be plenty of contractors involved. And that meant there'd be plenty of contracts. My father soon reported for duty with the colonel in charge at Fort Sam Houston.

"He gave me the rank of Captain and assigned me to work with the Lieutenant Colonel in charge of contracts," my father wrote. "In a few weeks, he retired and I was assigned to the job. Now my having taken that night school in law opened a big door. Our area of responsibility was the VII Corps Area, which covered most of Texas, except El Paso and the Texas Panhandle."

Clearly, the U.S. Army understood what every Texan already knew: that locations like El Paso and the Panhandle were closer to a lot of other places than they were to San Antonio. Between early 1942, when my father went on active duty, and the fateful events of early 1943, his territory would prove more than large enough and more than busy enough.

After his years with the Highway Department, in which the stated goal was to be fair, play by the rules and avoid political favoritism as much as possible, my father faced a new priority: Get the job done now, no matter what. With hindsight, I can see in his success with the Corps, in those feverish early days, the beginnings of what would attract a leader like General Leslie Groves to choose my father for the ultimate "Get the job done now, no matter what" assignment—the Manhattan Project.

In peacetime, there would be something questionable about the way Daddy described his dealings on twenty different military facilities while based out of Fort Sam Houston; in wartime, there was nothing questionable at all. "Projects were not formally advertised during this period and it was my assignment to informally invite certain contractors to bid on the various projects and negotiate the contract," he recorded.

My father's initial projects began near home. Even a fort like Sam Houston, which had been operational since the 1800s, needed considerable work to meet the needs generated by one world war with two far-flung theaters of operation, Europe and the Pacific. And the San Antonio area also became home to several air bases, still under the authority of what was called the U.S. Army Air Corps, which eventually found its own identity as today's U.S. Air Force. Each expansion demanded the very thing Elmer Calvin did best: contracts to build roads and streets, buildings of every type, water systems and sewage disposal. It wasn't always glamorous. But to produce each military "city" not only for the GIs but for their wives and children, it needed to be done, done right and done fast.

And then there was the single biggest job he handled in Texas during those years. The Army found and acquired 108,000 acres near Killeen west of Temple and decided to name what would be built there after a colorful adopted Texan, Confederate General John Bell Hood. Looking back at my father's carefully numbered sequence of needs there—1. Roads and streets, 2. Underground utilities, 3. Buildings, 4. Paving and surface treatment—I see why Camp Hood would become his *second*-greatest testament to how much a huge number of American officers, engineers and laborers could accomplish when their lives and freedom were at stake.

The area around today's Fort Hood (as early as 1943, that initial 108,000 acres grew to 158,000) has a long history of strife—a fact surely appropriate to the mood at the time of my father's arrival. In both European and Pacific theaters, U.S. soldiers were struggling to hold their own with huge losses of life and equipment. The Germans were winning most of the battles in faraway-sounding places like North Africa, and the Japanese were advancing from island to island in the Pacific. Such violence, though, was nothing new to the land soon to sprout 5,630 military buildings and house upwards of 100,000 soldiers and their families.

As usual, the area's earliest settlers were Native Americans—Apaches, Comanches, Kiowas and other tribes—but these were eventually caught in a squeeze play as the land ownership moved from Mexico to the Texas Republic to the United States. Fort Gates was set up to protect settlers, which Central Texas so severely needed, and by 1875 the cavalry had driven the tribes back far enough the newcomers could enjoy peace—briefly. Since cattle were the main profit centers, rustling them soon became a major industry. The locals didn't take it well. In 1874, the sheriff arrested some accused cattle rustlers and locked them in the jail in Belton to await trial. Instead, about a hundred locals broke into the jail and killed the prisoners. By tradition, this action scared would-be cattle rustlers badly enough that they gave up their bad habits or took them someplace else.

With the start of World War II, and specifically with the successes in Europe and North Africa of the Nazi tank Panzer units, Lieutenant Colonel Andrew D. Bruce figured it was time to, literally, fight fire with fire. The idea of "tank destroyers" won wide approval up and down the line: mobile anti-tank guns mounted on armored halftracks. After all, World War I had given us the so-called Machine Gun Center. Bruce and others felt World War II needed a Tank Destroyer Center, and its thirty-five firing ranges ended up being constructed by my father and his compatriots in central Texas at Camp Hood.

Dressed in civilian clothes to avoid arousing suspicion, Bruce and his assistants toured the Killeen area only two weeks after Pearl Harbor. And only a few days after that, the Army formally announced the Tank Destroyer Center would be located in what would become Camp Hood. In a somber foreshadowing of the Manhattan Project in Oak Ridge, Tennessee, this decision involved land purchases that would displace hundreds of local families. As a result, tiny communities with names like Clear Creek, Elijah, Antelop and Sugar Loaf ceased to exist. My father's friends back at the Highway Department immediately started building heavy-duty roads to the site, so construction equipment could make it in ahead of weaponry and fighting men. In keeping with the frenzied pace of that period, the Tank Destroyer and Firing Center moved from a temporary location to Camp Hood on August 2, 1942, with the camp officially opening less than a month after that.

Thanks to the camp's lively newspaper, called the *Hood Panther*, we have a portrait of what it was like to be an engineer building Camp Hood—and eventually a soldier serving there. In early 1943, for instance, there's an article headlined "Hood Men Must Be Clean—Electric, Sewage Conservation Needed." Citing the axiom that "cleanliness is next to godliness," the article talks about the two million gallons of water used by the camp each day, which arrived through eighty miles of water lines at an annual cost of $300,000.

In details about an infrastructure my father helped put in place, the news story also talks about the 250 miles of power lines that kept 210,000 electric devices functioning, including

600 refrigerators. In a bit of even less romantic information, there's mention of the camp's sixty miles of sewage lines carrying off a total of ninety-four million gallons of waste during a recent three-month period. During that same three months, the article states, the roads and grounds department rebuilt fourteen bridges, repaired eighteen others, fixed five miles of fence and salvaged about 400,000 feet of lumber. It had also maintained 150 miles of gravel and stabilized roadways while hauling off 2,500 tons of trash. "Aim of the post engineer organization," the article concludes, "is to operate all utilities as efficiently and effectively as possible and to maintain them so there will be no interruption of service. Members of the organization face the same problems in servicing the camp that a utility system does in caring for a city of 100,000 people."

Over the years of World War II, as the Tank Destroyer Center was augmented by the Infantry Replacement Training Center in March 1944, as the Allies prepared for the assault on Europe, there were surely many generals and other military celebrities who paid visits to Camp Hood. But if you skim through issues of the *Panther*, none seems quite so Texas-worthy as an officer in training there, Old West novelist Louis L'Amour.

In its feature story, the paper can barely contain its hero-worship: "Soldier, adventurer, fighter, writer and poet, that's Candidate Louis L'Amour of the 24th Officer Candidate School Class... A merchant seaman, a miner, a lumberjack, a tourist guide in Egypt, a soldier in the Chinese Civil Wars, a prize fighter, who fought in rings in more than one odd corner of the world, Candidate L'Amour has worked in the mines of Arizona and Nevada, on the docks of San Pedro and in the saw mills and lumber woods of Oregon." Ever patriotic, the article says L'Amour was "eager to write another chapter in his colorful life—a chapter of final victory for the Allies in their war against the dictators."

Long before this, however, my father's largest tasks at Camp Hood were done. After all, you couldn't train and house GIs until the construction was finished, and you couldn't construct until the contracts were negotiated and signed. In early 1943, Washington asked the commander of Fort Sam Houston to send five engineers with the appropriate skills to Dallas for a meeting with a general. My father and four others were selected and told to report to General Groves in a remote part of Tennessee the Army had started calling Oak Ridge.

➔ *Lillie, Elmer, Carolyn and Robert*

When in doubt, my father's engineering brain always listed things in order and assigned them numbers. I have to love the way he recorded his memory of that first meeting with General Groves in a simple frame building in Oak Ridge, since nothing else existed there yet.

"He told us: 1. Our project is called Manhattan, and is secret. 2. You know nothing of its purpose. 3. You will have many letters and calls asking you what are you doing. The answer is 'heavy construction.' 4. If you get in trouble here, and I need to release you, it will not be to the front lines. It will be as far away as possible. 5. Office and housing space is now under way for your purpose. 6. Dismissed."

BUILDING
The Bomb

CHAPTER FIVE

To his most recent biographer, writing at the dawn of the 21st century, General Leslie R. Groves was the "indispensable man" of the Manhattan Project that ended World War II and gave birth to the modern, dangerous Atomic Age. To me, however, General Groves was the smiling fellow in uniform, in the framed black-and-white photo my father kept on the wall of our den, complete with a personal inscription. "To Major E.B. Calvin," the general wrote, "in appreciation for what you did to make Manhattan Project a success."

There were a lot of good reasons that General Groves was a hero around our house. First and foremost because he *was* one. His management of the dizzying engineering mission that produced the bombs tested at Alamogordo, New Mexico, and then dropped on the Japanese cities of Hiroshima and Nagasaki indisputably saved tens of thousands of lives—including many lives in Japan—compared with the fire bombings of cities that would have continued and the planned land invasion that would have come. There was another reason General Groves was our hero, though, and why his photo still has a place of honor in my living room: like my father, he was an engineer. And thanks to him, my father the engineer found himself working on what must have been the largest engineering job in human history.

After the Japanese surrender, there were more than enough

accounts by some people involved (as General Groves slowly backed away from his obsession with secrecy that had kept even his wife and daughter from having a clue) and of course by journalists then and historians now. Yet as the months and then years passed, something strange and, I think, sad happened. It must have been the spirit of the age, the spirit that turned balding, bespectacled scientists into rock stars and paved the way for our worship of NASA a bit later; the engineers of the Manhattan Project were all too quickly forgotten.

That's why I think of the word "building" when I think of the bomb. General Groves, my father and many other faithful members of their beloved Corps of Engineers didn't dream up the bomb, didn't write a formula for the bomb, didn't draw a diagram of the bomb. They built it, because to actually end the war, somebody had to.

I was only four years old when those two bombs came tumbling out of the skies over Japan, the first of several that Groves and Co. had in the works should the Emperor not come to his senses. Happily, General Groves was working at peace the other way too, dropping leaflets all over the Empire urging citizens to rise up and demand unconditional surrender. This was obviously hard and bitter for the Japanese, with their ancient feelings about personal and national honor. Yet good sense, and the bomb, did prevail. The joy of V-J Day was felt across the civilized world, even as it prepared the way, using the same atomic technology and lots more like it, for the tensions of the Cold War.

I wish I could tell you my father kept detailed notes of his work on the Manhattan Project, particularly during his extended posting in Oak Ridge, Tennessee. But for one thing, the secrecy of this mission was such that anyone caught doing anything of the sort would have been in big trouble. Disclosing the project's secrets was punishable by up to ten years in prison and fines the equivalent of $129,000 today. Still, even more so, the "compartmentalization" General Groves enforced at Oak Ridge, as well as at the Hanford facility in Washington and the Los Alamos laboratory in New Mexico, was so intense that it's hard to say, at any given moment, what my father knew.

Over the years between the Japanese surrender and his death, my father occasionally alluded to the Manhattan Project, dropping some enticing hints about building the "gaseous diffusion plant." But for the most part, he let his experiences remain his memories alone. Now those memories are gone.

I've managed to clarify a few things in my own mind, concerning my father's participation and the building of the bomb in general. In a real sense, he was one of 600,000 Americans who "comprised or directly supported" the effort (that's General Groves' number, from his memoir published in 1962). For another, General Groves clearly understood the unavoidable disconnect between theory and practice, the natural conflict between the physicists who first fantasized about how such a bomb might exist, and the engineers charged with not only producing it but doing so on a heart-wrenching deadline. From a military standpoint, the job my father and his fellow engineers were given was indeed a race. And everyone who would have died had the war dragged on for weeks or months or years was alive because the race was won.

Into his final years, my father kept a letter dated May 2, 1944, and stamped CONFIDENTIAL among his personal papers,

→ *Oak Ridge panorama*

written to his Corps of Engineers boss John Flaherty from the War Manpower Commission and the Under Secretary of War. Though for the most part, workers and even labor unions in Oak Ridge cooperated with the Manhattan Project on the basis of patriotism, the letter assures anyone reading it that not all was smooth sailing. "This project is above that of any other activity," it states. "You and your associates have been assigned to the Clinton Engineer Works in order to insure that the completion of this project is not delayed as a result of any unsolved labor problems." Again, a few lines farther down: "Nothing must interfere with the effectuation of appropriate measures necessary to the attainment of this objective."

In all the years I had with my father after the destruction of Hiroshima and Nagasaki, he never once expressed a single regret. We enlightened moderns might look back on that day and find such sentiments racist or worse: not caring about fellow human beings because they happened to be Japanese. And yes, many of the dead were civilians, not combatants. Yet I now understand that my father's thoughts and feelings on the matter paralleled those of his mentor, and probably of many who lived through the war and lost one or more loved ones.

It wasn't hatred exactly, though evidence that Germans and Japanese were hated during the conflict is not very hard to find. It was probably a combination of sadness and absolute determination. The men and women of the Manhattan Project had been given a big job to do. And though almost none of them knew enough to know this at the time, the future of the entire world was counting on their ability to do it.

It was early 1943 when Elmer reported for duty as Design and Construction Engineer for General Groves in Oak Ridge— or, more accurately, at the Clinton Engineer Works east of

Knoxville, around which the town of Oak Ridge would spring up. It is clear from the historical record, however, that even with many "compartments" and many sub-commanders around the facility, it was General Groves himself who was in charge. That came through loud and clear in anything my father ever shared about the project.

History tells us that General Groves came to his role in 1942 after a career as a military engineer that convinced many he was as ready as anyone could be. Most recently, he had overseen construction of a new War Department building overlooking the Potomac River, a mammoth military city that could provide offices for the tens of thousands gathering to manage the European and Pacific wars. Today we know that building as the Pentagon. Before that, General Groves had directed construction of bases and other Army facilities valued at eight billion dollars that might have placed him in contact with my father. And before that, he had handled difficult assignments within the Corps of Engineers for *his* mentor, Colonel Ernest "Pot" Graves. The life lessons General Groves learned from Colonel Graves are evident in how the general's son Richard, who later became his biographer, described him after his death in 1970:

> "He was determined to succeed in everything he undertook. He played to win; he had no use for losers; moral victories did not exist for him. He took great pride in accomplishing those things that he thought worthwhile; to his way of thinking they were the fundamental virtues."

Biographer Robert S. Norris put it even more simply at the dawn of a new millennium: "There have been few people in this world who equaled the genius of Leslie Richard Groves for getting things done."

What came to be recognized as the biggest job of my father's career actually did begin with physicists, many European, either working in American university research facilities or trying to escape Europe as the Nazi curtain dropped. By the late 1930s, they had begun to see that the atom—long treated as the smallest particle of all matter—might be split, and that doing so would theoretically unleash immense amounts of energy. They weren't sure, in the beginning, how that might be done, or even what use to the world it might be. But the splitting worked in their calculations.

With the globe at war, it didn't take long for reports of any such breakthrough to reach military minds, and the notion of a weapon, an atomic bomb, quickly took hold at the highest levels. Meetings were held, papers written and read. As some of the physicists had escaped from Germany itself, there were reasonable fears that the Nazis were working on such a bomb—and possibly the Japanese as well. In his later years, General Groves would reflect on that situation and reassert that the "right side" had won the race for the bomb. Then, with an eye toward the Soviet Union, he maintained that if an aggressive, evil power had developed the bomb first and alone, that power would dominate the world "completely and immediately." To General Groves, the fact that the United States made no effort to do so, when it alone had the bomb, was proof enough of his moral assertion.

In a stroke of his signature style, General Groves was on his way to the Oak Ridge area the day after he was appointed to run the Manhattan Project. First up: acquiring the real estate for a plant larger than anything most men and women had ever seen. The area, like others drawn into the project, was remote—the fear of a nuclear mishap shaped every aspect of the government's initial thinking. Still, it was close enough to Knoxville to have an available, trainable work force. And surely best of all, from my father's point of view, Oak Ridge was all about the engineering.

Early on, the lab at Los Alamos became the home of physics

and the physicists. Therefore, it too was essential to the mission's eventual success. Yet in many ways, Los Alamos was the place General Groves of the Corps of Engineers felt least at home. There was, first, the matter of academic discipline: General Groves was not a physicist, and he quickly deduced that they respected only each other. He tried to reassure them early on that, while he knew little about physics, he did know how to do calculus. By all accounts, they were equal parts entertained and outraged. And then, as though that clear divide weren't bad enough, there was General Groves' well-documented distrust of anyone who was not American, as he defined it.

In addition to already hating our alleged war allies in Stalin's Soviet Union, he never got along well with the British, partners in the Manhattan Project. And his thoughts about the French ran even darker. I especially love one story I heard about General Groves walking in on some Italian physicists speaking in their native tongue. They'd have to go outside, the general informed them, if they wanted to speak *Hungarian.*

In keeping with his expertise, my father was ordered to Oak Ridge to construct a building. A very *large* building. On the Army's initial 56,000 acres of land and the 3,000 more that were acquired later, my father's job was to build a structure that eventually went by the name K-25. It was to be four-stories tall and half-a-mile long, in the shape of a U. The design included fifty-four contiguous buildings divided into nine sections, within which were cells of six stages—in some ways, a box with a box inside, and a smaller box inside of that, etc. Clearly, this enormous, odd building was created for some extremely specific purpose. And I'd say "gaseous diffusion" was about as specific as a purpose needed to get.

I can't really master what's called Graham's Law, which states that the rate of effusion of a gas is inversely proportional to the square root of its molecular mass. This law dictated that if you hold a mixture of two gases in a box with a semi-permeable membrane, the lighter molecules will pass from the container faster than the heavier. If there could be a series (or "cascade") of such boxes, or so this thinking went, each stage along the route would hold a more enriched mixture. This process, hardly tested, much less mastered even on a small scale in a lab, produced "gaseous diffusion." It also, according to the best minds within the Manhattan Project, seemed the most promising way to get the enriched uranium needed for a successful atomic bomb.

In the system used to build the bomb—mirroring the system used for many larger Corps of Engineers projects—a series of private contractors handled much of the work under command by the government, usually meaning General Groves. In the case of K-25, that meant a construction contract for M.W. Kellogg, which created a separate corporate identity called Kellex; continued contracts with universities, including Columbia, and a final, crucial agreement with Kellex, the Bell Telephone Laboratories and the Bakelite Corp. created a barrier that would be strong, porous and resistant to corrosion by the gas that had to be used, uranium hexaflouride. There were, in my father's Oak Ridge, many Indians. Happily, there was only one chief, whose inscribed photograph still resides in my living room.

Within the General Groves household, as within obviously thousands of others, my mother and I had little to no awareness of the nature of my father's work. As a military family, all we knew is that my mother, an aunt and I had been moved somewhere for a new assignment. The government built us a three-bedroom house in this town that previously hadn't even existed. I was only two when the move happened so I remember little of the years at Oak Ridge.

Not surprisingly, there was quite a strong feeling of community among families living in this strange place with only each other to rely upon. I still have a photo of me and a few other Oak Ridge kids, all boys as it turned out, sitting a table with our teacher at

→ *Carolyn and other kids at school in Oak Ridge*

nursery school.

Naturally, my personal memories of life in Oak Ridge are few and far between, but plenty of interesting things came down to me from Daddy, as well as from my later research. The land along the Clinch River about thirty miles from Knoxville was always a bastion of rural peace, going back to the years it was inhabited by the Cherokees and after its ownership passed into the hands of the white man. Generations lived on the land, so isolated that even big events like the Civil War, and much later the Great Depression, passed largely unnoticed. What didn't pass unnoticed, apparently, was also the area's weirdest moment ever.

A man named John Hendrix was born in the region in 1865 and grew up to consider himself a prophet. He was, by all accounts, just another subsistence-level farmer until his daughter died, and from that time he claimed to be in direct communication with the Almighty. And the Almighty seemed to be quite talkative when it came to the valley that eventually became Oak Ridge. "Bear Creek Valley someday will be filled with great buildings and factories and they will help toward winning the greatest war that will ever be…Big engines will dig big ditches and there will be great notice and confusion, and the earth will shake." I don't know what I think of John Hendrix as a prophet, but he certainly got a lot of the details right.

Later scholars have talked about the disruptive side of the government's work on the Manhattan Project, starting with the displacement of many long-term families from the land. There was a money aspect, only $34 to $44 per acre, paid to families to leave—and leave *now*. Some locals were offered jobs at the Manhattan Project, fairly low-level surely, and some of the younger people stayed on to work too. Thus, the world my family moved into was a strange one—traditional extended families shattered, lots of new people to meet (and in some cases marry), new bonds formed around work and friendship. Almost everybody, in other words, was a stranger, a newcomer.

In all, the rapidly built first phase of Oak Ridge featured 3,050 houses ranging from one- to three-bedrooms, three efficiency apartment buildings, seventeen 150-man dormitories, a fifty bed hospital and four schools. All the construction tried to make maximum use of the lovely hills and hollows, providing the best sense of well-being possible in the close quarters required.

Neighborhoods had sidewalks and access to public transportation, and homes were even built at angles to make them seem less close than they were. Shopping centers, churches and cultural amenities were all within walking distance of our house. It was "smart growth" as our country came to understand it in the years ahead—yet smart growth with a big, burning secret at its core.

Specifically, at Oak Ridge, my father ended up helping in a major way with the foundations for the gaseous diffusion plant. A lot of notions were being tossed around by the various Army engineers and the contractors working on the project, but my father suggested the way the job would be done if it were a *highway* back home in Texas. You'd put down a layer of crushed stone, and then you'd put a layer of reinforced concrete on top of that. The men at the table seemed satisfied with that idea, but the

→ *Bridge over Clinch River built by Elmer*

only crushed stone was on the far side of a large lake. Somebody would have to build a floating bridge, and that meant a whole new contractor to handle a whole new job—until, that is, my father heard about a supply of Mississippi River barges gathered in New Orleans from the region stretching from Texas to Florida.

Daddy caught a train south from Knoxville, located the barges, got approval from the colonel in charge and started a slow trip up the river with five barges in tow. Rather than build a permanent bridge across the lake, my father lined up the barges, stripped away anything that might get in the way, and used the connected barges to *be* his bridge for four tons of crushed stone. As my father recounted late in his life, General Groves and everybody else held their breath when the first overloaded truck started onto the first barge, which sank a couple inches lower in the lake but otherwise passed with flying colors. My father recalled someone shouting "Let her roll," meaning he had just managed to construct one of the fastest bridges in all human history.

My father was part of K-25 from the start in May 1943, when a survey party marked out the chosen site. Construction on the main building began less than six months later, with a six-stage pilot plant ready for operation by April. February 1945 saw the production plant rev up in stages, cascade after cascade, each step producing better enrichment than the one before. By early August, the last of the plant's 2,892 stages commenced operation.

As family history recounts it, my father's main job in Oak Ridge was engineering that gaseous diffusion plant. Yet a secondary role he played introduces a compelling mystery, especially after my efforts to track down facts. As the construction progressed, presumably taking on a life of its own, my father increasingly concerned himself with the search for uranium, and then plutonium. Strange as it may seem, with all the calculating going on, nobody knew exactly how much of the stuff would be needed to explode a single atomic bomb—much less how many bombs it would take to convince the Emperor to call it quits. Essentially, we needed all the uranium we could get our hands on, and for a time that became part of my father's job.

As it turns out, most of the uranium came from deep in the Belgian Congo, by way of a Belgian company later decorated for its service to freedom—and, like all the other private contractors, they were paid quite handsomely. My father told me he spent a good deal of 1945 in an office in Philadelphia, working with people at DuPont to corner the supply of

→ *Philadelphia, December 1945*

plutonium for use at the Hanford facility. That would have been for a third atomic bomb. Everyone involved was relieved when we didn't have to drop one.

Strangely perhaps—but then again, the Manhattan Project was a secret—we have nothing in our family's remembered history beyond the fact that Mother and I, along with an aunt of hers, were moved to Philadelphia during the months Daddy was assigned there. I do have one memory, though, that points toward some sort of old, dark brownstone house. It was Halloween and as part of trick-or-treating I remember being passed from family to family along the porches. I don't believe there was any building of the sort tossed up overnight by the Army in Oak Ridge.

It's intriguing to find among my father's papers a copy of his letter to the Texas Highway Department dated June 20, 1945. The war in Europe had ended and the war in the Pacific was winding down, so his old bosses in Austin had not only offered my father a job but volunteered to lobby for his release from the Army. This was definitely a case of "little did they know," and Elmer Calvin wasn't in any situation to tell them.

"Some three weeks ago," he explained, "I made a request for a release and my Commanding Officer rejected the request, and

I have been given an assignment here in Philadelphia which is the most responsible job I have had since being in the Manhattan District. My title is Assistant to the District Engineer and, of course, due to the secrecy of our work, I cannot divulge the details of the assignments."

Some of those "details" came to fruition less than a month later, on July 16. As my father learned by unscrambling a coded three-word message that came into his office in Philadelphia, the atomic bomb was no longer just a physicist's equation.

"It was successful."

That's all the message said. The "it" was the first successful test of what insiders had taken to calling "the gadget," initially planned for the Los Alamos area but moved to then even more remote Alamogordo section of New Mexico for safety reasons. That the no less a physicist than Enrico Fermi joked about the possibility that the world might blow up is notable, though it now seems he was only trying to break the tension. General Groves was on hand for the test, code named Trinity—as was Oppenheimer and perhaps three-hundred others in the project's inner circle. These were not just VIPs, and since no one could be sure of the outcome, these were people of specific disciplines who could observe the blast and quickly do calculations about what it meant to a planned use on the other side of the world, now as little as two weeks away.

All these decades later, it's still hard for me to imagine anything more dramatic than the brief flash (described as being "equal to several suns at midday") followed by the now-iconic purplish mushroom cloud rising high into the New Mexico sky. Even Texas had a role to play in Trinity, since some of the earliest outside reports of this mysterious explosion came via the news media in El Paso. An initial press release approved by General Groves blamed the event on a "remotely located ammunition magazine." Lulled almost to sleep by such mundane news, the world was in for quite a shock in the hours and days to come.

Four of the first words General Groves heard from the man he'd put in charge of Trinity, General Thomas Farrell, were, "The war is over." Given a little distance from the moment, though, Farrell would describe the test as "the birth of a new age." And he would resort to his Catholic upbringing to describe what followed that flash: "the strong, sustained awesome roar which warned of doomsday and made us feel that we puny things were blasphemous to dare tamper with the forces heretofore reserved to The Almighty."

With my father holding his breath, along with all the other insiders at Los Alamos, Hanford and elsewhere in the Manhattan Project, the B-29 bomber *Enola Gay* of the 393rd Bombardment Squadron took off from the Pacific island of Tinian on August 6, 1945, its primary target an army depot and port called Hiroshima. The bomb known as Little Boy detonated at 1,750 feet above the ground, virtually flattening 4.7 square miles of the city, killing 70,000-80,000 people and injuring 70,000 more. Three days later, the B-29 *Bockscar* lifted off from Tinian with a bomb called Fat Man. Cloud cover turned its secondary target into its primary, and Nagasaki entered the history books. Some 35,000 people perished in the swirling atomic blast, with 60,000 more injured. World War II was effectively over. A frightening new era in world history had begun.

"An answer to the question, 'Was the development of the atomic bomb by the United States necessary,'" General Groves would write in his own Manhattan Project memoir, "I reply unequivocally, 'Yes.' To the question, 'Is atomic energy a force for good or evil?' I can only say, 'As mankind wills it.'"

LONE STAR
Return

CHAPTER SIX

After the end of World War II, my parents made their way to Dallas by interstate highway—in a sense that was more literal than many of us might even today. But that didn't happen before my father received a very kind letter from the U.S. Army Corps of Engineers.

"Your recent release from active duty," wrote Colonel K.D. Nichols, District Engineer for Oak Ridge, "marks the culmination of almost three and one-half years of service to your country during wartime. You have occasion to be proud of this service." After detailing several key elements of my father's work, both in Tennessee and later in Pennsylvania, Colonel Nichols wished my father a bright post-military future. "I wish you every possible success as you resume your civilian career and return to your work in Texas."

The colonel clearly was in possession of certain facts about my father's plans, but maybe not in possession of others. My father would indeed, like many GIs given honorable discharges, eventually be returning to his pre-war employer, the Texas Highway Department—even if it was after two years with a private construction company. Still, it wasn't anybody's "return" to move to the city of Dallas, where we had never lived, not to mention the largest metropolis in which we would ever truly put down roots.

And before long, it was clear my father wasn't "returning" to

→ *New highway into Dallas*

precisely the same kind of work he had done in Albany or Austin. In his old resume that I've kept, dry and yellowed after all these years, Daddy talks about working in and around Dallas on all types of highways, from farm-to-market to "super expressways." He didn't quite employ the term that would soon come into constant use, but the Age of the American Interstate was upon us.

Interestingly, the next phase of my father's career and our family's life is evident now looking back at a series of letters exchanged from Philadelphia with District Engineer D. E. H. Manigault of Austin. I can't exactly tell what was on my father's mind, and he certainly doesn't say in these letters but it seems he was having an internal tug-of-war between staying until the last details of the Manhattan Project were complete, and getting back to Texas ahead of the GIs everybody knew would soon be coming home to get jobs.

On August 9, for instance, my father writes that he'd been in Washington that same week and "this matter was discussed in detail" and that he'd been assured his commanding officer would give his discharge "favorable attention" in October. Only eight days later, however, he is writing Manigault again, saying that V-J

Day appears to be "right around the corner" and that it might be possible to return to work before October. There were the trappings of an expected promotion, he says, but "I would gladly sacrifice those things if you have some assignment for me that you cannot hold open until October."

The two letters from Manigault in my father's file reflect considerable respect and affection. "I am very glad that we may expect you soon," the district engineer writes on August 31. Yet he also grabs the opportunity to worry about money: "We have four field engineers and three helpers that show promise. How will we get enough skilled helpers to do our field work? As a general thing wages are on the up and up. As yet we are not prepared to meet them. Some of the veterans expect fantastic salaries. What will be the upshot?" Before my father could think too hard about whether Manigault was playing employer hardball, another letter arrived saying the engineer had been pressured into retiring. It was a "shock," Manigault admits, and "a little sooner than I had expected...I am quite sure that the State Highway Department will carry out their obligation to all returning servicemen and that you can count on a good job."

Maybe that *was* the story within these letters, that with money tight and GIs coming home (expecting "fantastic salaries," no less), it was in my father's interest to get home to Texas sooner rather than later. After all, he had a wife and daughter to support.

Somewhere in all that may reside the reason Elmer Calvin's move to Dallas in December 1945 did not take him immediately to the Highway Department but to Grafe-Callahan Construction, and one happy side effect was that our family finally found a true home. From the end of 1945 until my parents' deaths they would consider themselves Dallas residents. And even after many years of work in foreign countries, even after I'd grown up and moved away, the Calvin house on Beverly Drive in Highland Park remained the home we could all come home to.

Today, when people talk about the interstate system, in Texas or anyplace else, the name of one U.S. president invariably comes up: Dwight D. Eisenhower. In many ways, the system of expressways connecting the farthest-flung corners of the republic was Eisenhower's baby. After several years of making childish (but successful) generals work together to defeat the Nazis, he was apparently ready to use the same glue on local, state and national politicians to the get the roads he felt the nation needed. And of course, there were plenty of great reasons we did.

The concept of "national roads" was nothing new—the term was used by Thomas Jefferson when he approved such a thing back in 1803. But frankly, not until World War II—when as my father knew better than almost anyone, each new military construction required new roads to reach it—did most observers see advantages in connecting points east, west, north and south. And remember, the Cold War standoff with the Soviet Union began almost the second Germany and, finally, Japan surrendered. Sadly, it didn't seem outlandish to picture another war making another set of Elmer Calvins build another set of military installations, in a hurry.

Still, even if calmer heads prevailed—as they generally did, citing the cataclysmic impact of the atomic weapons waved about by both sides—there were advantages to better transportation in the boom that followed the war. For one thing, returning GIs were marrying and having children with unforeseen intensity, giving us the so-called Baby Boom. This demand invited supply, colored in those years by a new and some would say dangerous emphasis on low-cost consumer goods that an earlier generation didn't have and didn't need. And Charles M. Upham was proved right: increasing shares of those consumer goods traveled by truck over the nation's roads, rather than on rails, fueling the commerce that became the American economy. Better roads would make such transport faster and more efficient, not to mention safer, decreasing costs and losses while keeping the 1950s American housewife happy indeed.

Finally, interstates (or my father's "super expressways") created something I'm not one hundred percent sure anyone fully foresaw. Better roads created the opportunity for returning GIs, with affordable mortgage loans via the VA, to live farther and farther from their work in the downtown areas of growing Texas cities like Dallas-Fort Worth and Houston, Austin and San Antonio. Yes,

→ *Texas highway visionary Dewitt Greer*

by building expressways and connecting them into the interstate system, my father and his peers at the Highway Department made it possible for urban areas to have suburban and exurban areas. And that, of course, would change everything.

It wasn't my father but certainly a Texan within his department who came up with an iconic design that would become familiar to millions of Americans. Richard Oliver, a senior traffic engineer, submitted one of a hundred-plus concepts that would eventually be narrowed down to four in 1956: one each from Texas, Louisiana and New Hampshire, plus one from the American Association of State Highway Officials. As Oliver expressed it some years later: "It never would have occurred to me to enter a design. But my boss said draw something, and it won." He submitted the design in simple black and white. Expressing pride "that Texas won this honor," famed State Highway Engineer Dewitt Greer (who figures in plenty of my father's later stories) notified Oliver that his work had been selected—and somewhere a factory started gearing up to spit out those red, white and blue metal shields that would mark interstates everywhere. Typical of the people my father always seemed to work with, Oliver took his instant "fame" in stride, even with the folks at his church. "Somehow the word got out," he remembered, "and I got requests to design our denomination's newsletter."

In spending two years with Grafe-Callahan, my father indulged in the most common career path of professionals who work with or within governments everywhere—taking their skills (and their Rolodex) outside for a while. With that single employment decision, my father went from soliciting bids and plans from construction companies to *creating* them for submission. Nobody can say he didn't know what the Highway Department was looking for. And in another common move, his two years with the construction firm—during which his efforts focused on building two plants for Hot Mix Asphaltic Concrete—made him all the more desirable to his old friends at the Highway Department, which made him a better offer to join the Dallas office in August 1947.

In a letter I've discovered from shortly before that, however, I see an additional element to my father's work in the private sector, one that prefigured the kind of jobs that would fill the final years of his career. The Public Roads Administration of the Federal Works Agency in the Philippines wrote to my father at Grafe-Callaghan about the pressing need for postwar reconstruction there, and the amount of money coming available to pay for it. In addition to two paving projects in Manila itself, the first phase of reconstruction would include several road assignments in the countryside, plus the repair and reconstruction of several bridges knocked on during the long Japanese occupation of the islands.

"Of course," wrote programming and planning engineer A.C. Taylor, "a contractor who is looking for a new field could obtain an initial advantage if he would send his own representative immediately...If you decide to send a man out here I suggest that you contact the Public Roads Administration in Washington."

On the one hand, there are inklings in this letter of the assignments my father would travel the world handling during his "foreign service" period. As far as I know, my father never went to the Philippines. And with Grafe-Callaghan now out of business for some years, I have no way to check if he ever "sent a man."

In America, in general, interstate highways were a long time coming—but when they did, with a bold assist from my father and his visionary Highway Department boss Greer, they came on with a vengeance. The first inkling of such a thing goes back to the war— World War I, that is—when a young U.S. soldier named Dwight D. Eisenhower took part in an exercise driving trucks and tanks from Washington, D.C. to San Francisco. As the journey lasted weeks, it was considered proof that America's hodgepodge of mostly poor roads represented a military risk.

→ *Miles and miles of Texas*

Eisenhower never forgot the lesson, though by the time our country entered World War II, there was no money available to improve roads. As early as 1944, the government envisioned a route system that would link all U.S. cities with populations of 300,000 or more, and even fifty-nine of the sixty-two cities with populations of 100,000 or more. Even though my father was still in the Army at the time, and then at Grafe-Callahan, state highway departments were asked to start filling in the details. By the time my father came to work for Greer, the story was moving ahead furiously. And that involved the three things my father did best: route selection, purchasing rights of way and hiring contractors. He was about to be part of another Texas highway golden age.

As any Texas driver knows all too well, the basic plan for auto transportation involves turning the largest cities—Dallas-Fort Worth, Houston, Austin and San Antonio—into hubs, then creating "spokes" that go out from there. Long stretches of interstate could then connect the cities, giving new life to once-isolated small towns along their route. Greer and his staff got off to an excellent start. With the federal government kicking in ninety percent of costs, and the states responsible for only ten percent, Texas accounted for no less than *twenty-five percent* of the total highway work in the entire United States in 1947. As one observer put it, Texas was becoming—both more, and more quickly, than any other state—a "civilization geared to motor vehicles."

According to a later Texas Highway Department memo, my father's specific achievements during this period included the development of Rockwall and "such adjacent county projects" as US-80 in Kaufman, US-75 in Collin, and twenty-eight miles of expressway surveys and other components for US-75 and US-77 in Ellis. Elmer Calvin, according to this document, "is most energetic and aggressive, with an excellent background in construction and plan work. He is a very hard worker, and enthusiastic in his work, never at any time night or day failing to give his work his highest undivided attention." As the man's daughter, I can only agree.

To understand what my father did from his home base in Dallas, you need to know something about Greer. In all, his department would spend $4.5 billion (today valued at $35.5 billion) without anybody saying he put a penny in the wrong pocket. It was said admiringly at the time that "a contractor couldn't buy him a cup of coffee," and that approach was very much part of my father's dealings as well.

Equally impressive, it was Greer's belief that all money should go "under the rubber"—roads beneath drivers' tires—not on various administrative costs that haunt so much government work. A slice of the pie that used to be thirty percent found itself trimmed to about *one percent* under Dewitt Greer. Considering the traditions of Texas politics, it speaks volumes that the department's motto under Greer was "Guts and Integrity."

Having learned how to make Texas highways work during

the Depression, Greer again built an operation that emphasized the benefit of near-total state control over federal funding. As a result, he left his fingerprints all over the interstate system in Texas, making it notably different in some specifics from the interstate system anywhere else. Admittedly, some differences became less pronounced over the years as more and more states adopted Texas innovations.

With his emphasis in the cities as hubs, Greer opened "expressway offices" in Austin, San Antonio, Houston and Dallas-Fort Worth as early as 1945, in addition to his department's regular "district" offices. He felt it essential that any major highway through a large Texas city be built from the start to connect to an interstate. Since individual cities paid almost nothing for these thoroughfares, they had extremely little say in the routes—often for better, though occasionally for worse.

Even today, anyone driving on interstates in Texas should recognize the most visible legacy of Greer's years running the highway department: frontage roads. In Dallas-Fort Worth, they came to be known as "service roads," as "access roads" in San Antonio, as "gateway roads" in El Paso, and as "feeder roads" in Houston, thus reflecting the autonomy of each urban highway office.

The main objective, for Greer, was not to produce roads only for people to go long distances across Texas without stopping. Exits were placed, in many cases, miles closer than they would have been elsewhere, with the frontage roads letting a stream of cars conveniently reach local businesses. His intent, shared with my father in his year-round negotiations to purchase rights-of-way, was for the highways to be positive forces in a local economy rather than negative ones. Despite a generation or two of urban or even suburban sprawl, there is no question that running an interstate through an area increased the property values for land that had convenient access hundreds or even thousands of times over. In time, Texas could boast some 4,500 miles of frontage road along its interstate highways and freeways.

Once in a while, that was the rub. When my father went forth to select an interstate route, three primary factors were on his mind: availability of right-of-way, meaning he could purchase land for the state affordably; how many homes or businesses would be displaced; and the anticipated economic impact. As the Texas interstate system became a physical reality, throughout my father's years with Greer's department, this latter component became a source of considerable heartache. At times, it seemed my father was destroying the state's very roadside culture that he and his highway coworkers had created during his first period with the state in the 1920s and 1930s.

Suddenly, even along the most iconic American roads like Route 66, there was virtually no life after the interstate passed you by. For instance, the town of McLean in the Panhandle had become a thriving enterprise with more than 1500 residents during the golden age of Route 66, with service stations, motels, cafes, six churches and fifty-nine businesses. The population had already begun to decline with the growth of Pampa and especially Amarillo, but its bypass by I-40 was the final blow.

Nearly all the businesses that lived off tourist traffic along Route 66 are now gone, even though the town still strives to attract those few travelers drawn by nostalgia. McLean, appropriately, is the headquarters of the Texas Historic Route 66 Association. Around the highway department, and indeed around my father's desk, everything was positive about progress in the late 1940s and early 1950s. Nobody in Texas knew the complete story yet: the highway giveth, and the highway taketh away.

As he recalled later, one of my father's specific mandates from Greer was to expand the department's network of highway contractors—a task nearly all of his work experience had prepared him for. Traditionally, of course, such contracts were parceled out to a short list of political cronies and contributors. However, with the advancements made in new construction technology during and since World War II, Texas was an innovator with pre-stressed concrete, slip-form pavement sections, asphalt binders, grooved pavement, better signage and computerized design. Daddy saw the opportunity, or the necessity, to look further and deeper than the local pol's dove hunting buddies. Even as he sought out the best companies, though, my father followed Greer's other instruction to spread smaller "packages" across qualified companies in each area. The reasons included local economic development, of course, but

→ *A new Texas bridge*

also the hiring of smaller firms to maintain the highways long after the main builders had finished and moved on.

As 1956 got serious after the holidays, my father viewed his second, nearly nine-year stint with the highway department with satisfaction—even as he had to regularly answer queries about when he might want to retire. Not only had he gotten to work alongside the legendary Dewitt Greer but he'd gotten to route, help design, solicit contractors and select bids for numerous Dallas-area roads with cute little names like, well, I-35 and I-20. He might retire, surely, with that amount of work behind him. Still, as it happens sometimes, such a record of success catches other people's eyes.

One former department employee, Conrad Kelley, by now working in the private sector, met Charles M. Upham at an industry event, and understood that Upham had just won a contract from the Egyptian government to assist and advise its fledgling roads program. Without missing a beat, this friend suggested my father's name to Upham, just in case he was looking for a construction engineer with a special talent for contractors and contracts. The rest is history. In fact, by the following Halloween, my father's first overseas assignment would be a great deal more history than any of us was bargaining for.

→ *I-35 across Brazos at Waco*

UNCLE
Earle

CHAPTER SEVEN

My mother had an adventurous spirit. So it was with that in 1955, while Daddy was still busy connecting North Texas to the world with interstate highways, the two of us traveled from Dallas to Japan to visit the one man on earth I admired (and even years after his passing, still admire) almost as much as I do my father. The trip was long and grueling, as most overseas trips were back then; but it let me finally, as a fourteen-year-old, get to know my Uncle Earle—the gifted military doctor who oversaw so much of the medical treatment given our troops during World War II and the Korean War, and who eventually retired as a two-star general.

→ *Earle Standlee*

The trip was quite an undertaking, because of the huge number of miles involved and also because of the destruction still left in some areas from World War II. While my mother and I were in Japan to visit her brother, Earle himself was away as much as he was there, whether running between various duties in Japan or slipping over to Korea to deal with its problems. That certainly didn't keep us from enjoying ourselves, however, whether that meant taking side trips to Kyoto to see so much Japanese cultural and religious history, or from pleasures as simple as going grocery shopping with Earle's two Japanese maids to prepare *sukiyaki* for us that evening.

Even when the Japanese visit was over, my mother and I took our time getting back to Dallas—stopping to see the sights in the then-British crown colony of Hong Kong before doing the same in and around Manila in the Philippines. The devastation of the war was still evident there, more than in Hong Kong and even more than in some parts of Japan.

By all accounts, Earle Standlee was especially close to my mother when they were young, and I suppose that was what made him so real to me when I was growing up—even though he was often stationed far away. Earle's own life adventures—in Europe during World War II and in Japan during the Korean War—enriched the backdrop that my early life was projected against. In other words, the world was a place you actually *went* in your life, not just someplace you read about in books or watched in movies or later on television. I came to admire Uncle Earle and saw him and my Aunt Mary as often as I could once they had retired from the Army to Dallas. I even lived with them for a time.

Considering the belief in education on both sides of my family, it goes without saying that Earle went to college, earning his bachelor's degree at Baylor in Waco in 1920 (only months before my father started at A&M). After a brief stint of his own in teaching, Earle signed on at the Baylor Medical School, finished his M.D. in 1925 and joined the military. As best we can tell, it was an interesting time to do so, close enough to the end of World War I that people weren't paying the Army much attention anymore. World War I, at the time, was known as the "War to End All Wars."

As a doctor, Earle's military assignments were typically based at military hospitals, in the states and overseas, where all the typical things civilian doctors did were done by military doctors. Shortly after joining the Army, for instance, Earle was stationed in San Antonio and living in a boarding house. Another of the residents was named Mary Walker, a pretty young school teacher with both a B.A. and an M.A. from the University of Texas. The two fell in love and got married just about the time Earle's superiors were cooking up an exotic assignment for him, practicing Army medicine as Chief of Medical Service at Fort McKinley in Manila, the capital of the Philippines.

Years before the Empire of the Rising Sun, this was a great adventure for the young couple. As Uncle Earle and Aunt Mary remembered it later, they lived in Manila in a "tent," the conditions incredibly rustic, creature comforts few and far between. When we youngsters would ask them why, all they'd say is they were saving money to buy some beautiful Chinese rugs. These rugs would be one of the Standlee family's enduring legacies. While still stationed at Fort McKinley, Earle and Mary were blessed with their first child, a boy named Earle Glenn Jr.

Around 1930, the Army brought the Standlees home to Washington, D.C., giving Uncle Earle the first of many staff positions he would hold during the rest of his career. This one was at Walter Reed, the legendary military hospital, which also

➔ *Scene from Army Hospital in Tokyo*

hired Aunt Mary to serve as its librarian. Stationed there through the years leading up to World War II, Earle and Mary expanded the family, with Wanda in 1930 and another boy, Ranald Rhey, in 1932. The Standlees lived within walking distance of the hospital.

The kids had all the benefits of growing up in a military family in the nation's capital, with regular forays to Congress, the White House and the Smithsonian. During those years Earle became known as an expert internist, a diagnostician, rather than a surgeon. We all remember Aunt Mary bragging on her husband just a little, since Earle was much too quiet and modest to brag on himself. "He's the one," she often said, "who tells the surgeons what to do." During this time, my cousin Wanda reminds me, he also commuted up to Cambridge, Massachusetts, to earn a graduate degree in business administration from Harvard in 1941.

With the buildup to the war in Europe and the sudden attack on Pearl Harbor, the American military changed overnight—and it was understood, though not discussed much in public, that doctors would have their hands full very soon. In preparation for what promised to be a lengthy conflict, Earle and Mary sent their two younger children to live with Mary's parents in the country outside Hillsborough, Texas. Because their eldest child was considered "sickly" he was kept at home until he could be sent to Valley Forge Military Academy. Mary remained in Washington, working at Walter Reed, starting to amass the mountains of historical information about the hospital that would play an important role in her later life.

Sometime late in 1942, the Army sent Uncle Earle to what was known as the "European Theater"—even though the earliest major battles weren't actually in Europe at all. At the highest levels, decisions were made that focused on North Africa, where German General Irwin Rommel (known as the "Desert Fox") had inflicted horrifying defeats on both our British allies and on young American forces struggling to get organized.

It was about this time that war correspondent Thomas R. Henry caught up with Earle "near the Tunisian front," as military censorship dictated for vague datelines in those days. In his dispatch for the North American Newspaper Alliance, Henry described a full-scale hospital Earle had just set up in the desert, complete with a staff of fifty-six doctors, 105 nurses and 500 enlisted men. The correspondent added that the unit was built with 600 tons of equipment brought in, just in time to treat 1500 patients sent to the hospital's seven operating rooms from some of the worst of the fighting some miles away.

"Almost entirely under canvas," wrote Henry, "the hospital is a model of military cleanliness, efficiency and discipline. It is one of the few stations in the Army where saluting is rigidly required of nurses."

Meanwhile, back at Allied headquarters, General Eisenhower decided to send in a fellow West Point graduate who many felt could get the job done. That officer was General George S. Patton Jr. Beginning with the North Africa campaign, first as Deputy Surgeon North African Theatre, and later as Chief Surgeon Mediterranean Theatre, my Uncle Earle would serve as a crucial medical officer for Patton's now-legendary success.

After the general's impressive victory over Rommel's troops at El Guettar, sustained efforts in tank battle after tank battle pushed the Germans against General Bernard Law Montgomery's British Eighth Army, until thousands of the enemy died, surrendered or escaped from North Africa altogether. At that point, the focus switched to Italy, where of course Mussolini had formed the most significant alliance with Hitler that World War II would produce. Beginning as far south in Italy as anyone could get, on the island of Sicily, Uncle Earle followed Patton mile after mile to the north.

As the officer in charge of setting up hospitals for Patton's troops, Uncle Earle was front and center for the most contro-

→ *Young Japanese girls*

→ *Agnes and Earle at Camp Zama*

versial chapter in the general's career. On not one but two occasions, General Patton was visiting wounded troops in Sicily and encountered GIs who were "nervous" about returning to the front lines. "I guess I can't take it," the first of these soldiers admitted to his commanding officer, who had been known since North Africa as "Old Blood and Guts." At this point, General Patton slapped the young man across the face, an action he repeated with a similar patient a short time later.

→ *Earle honored for his service*

Since Earle was a medical doctor, he probably knew a great deal more about what we now call "post-traumatic stress disorder"—though it didn't have that official name for years. Earle did, however, have to suffer through the international media spotlight turned on General Patton when U.S. syndicated newspaper columnist Drew Pearson reported details of the "Slapping Incident." Many inside the military, and naturally out of it, demanded that General Patton be fired.

To his credit, I think, Eisenhower did his best to balance conflicting interests. As a lifelong military man, he did consider General Patton's actions a serious betrayal of the Army's written procedures and unwritten codes of honor. Yet he also knew that he had in General Patton the Allies' single most aggressive and effective weapon against the Nazi war machine. The general was forced to apologize to the men he slapped and endure a time in his own wilderness as the European war seemed to go forward without him, first with the conquest of Italy and then with preparations for the life-or-death assault on the French coast at Normandy that the world would come to know as D-Day.

It was during this fallow period that my uncle turns up in U.S. military history, meeting at the university in Algiers with other doctors from the three principal Allies: the United States,

Great Britain and France. As a report called the *American Letter* points out, "They were one of the largest groups of medical men ever to confer overseas. Colonel Earle Standlee led the U.S. delegation." One entire day of the conference, we're told, was reserved for a discussion of typhus, while the other two days covered diseases and injuries common to warfare.

Though Uncle Earle and his commander could not have predicted it at the time, General Patton's ten months of inactivity proved something of a godsend to the Normandy invasion. The fact that the man the German high command viewed as America's chief weapon stayed on in Sicily convinced them the invasion would come via southern France. And the fact that General Patton spent some of 1944 in Cairo led the enemy to prepare for an invasion by way of the Balkans. Nazi documents now tell us that Hitler's upper echelon followed the general's every move and remade their defense to respond to each one.

Neither General Patton nor my Uncle Earle would go ashore on those Normandy beaches of June 6, 1944. Though the German defenses there were well entrenched and undeniably brutal, a notable portion of their strength had been diverted to attack General Patton—wherever the great combat general chose to invade.

It wasn't long, though, before the new Third Army joined the fight. It formed around General Patton on August 1, its initial assignment known as Operation COBRA to blast the Allies out of the tight hedgerows of northern France and get them moving toward liberating Nazi-occupied Paris, crossing the Rhine River from France into Germany and finally capturing or killing the last Nazi standing in Berlin.

With Uncle Earle administering the hospitals, the fast forward motion that made General Patton famous presented its own almost unimaginable medical challenges. As part of Operation COBRA, for instance, the Third Army attacked Nazi forces west, east, north and south—all at the same time. And General Patton was known for never slowing down to let other parts of his operation catch up. The moment was too crucial, he believed, and the advantage too expensive in terms of his men's blood.

"Whenever you slow anything down," he once said, "you waste human lives." It was up to others—my Uncle Earle among them—to figure out where to actually treat the GIs who fell during the Third Army's sometimes crazy, always relentless crusade across Europe.

Between the time it became operational and the German surrender on May 9, 1945, Third Army was in continuous combat for 281 days. It advanced farther and faster than any army in military history, crossing twenty-four major rivers and capturing 81,500 square miles of territory, including more than 12,000 cities and towns in France, Belgium, Luxembourg, Germany, Austria and Czechoslovakia. The Third killed, wounded, or captured no fewer than 1,811,388 enemy soldiers, six times its strength in personnel. As a comparison, General Patton's army suffered 16,596 killed; 96,241 wounded; and 26,809 missing in action. At one point, Earle was the only survivor of a ship sunk by the German Navy in the middle of the Mediterranean. He floated for days before his rescue.

After May 9, 1945 went into the history books as Victory in Europe (V-E) Day, Earle spent the years until the Korean War at the Pentagon and then at nearby Fort Monroe in Virginia. The Army was clearly grooming him for some of the highest responsibilities it had to offer, promoting him in rank and increasing his areas of oversight, first as Surgeon of the Army Field and, by 1951, as chief of the Planning Coordination Division of the Armed Forces Medical Policy Council. With the ongoing reconstruction of Japan after Hiroshima and Nagasaki, and with war erupting again in Korea, those responsibilities awaited my uncle during three years in Japan. On July 26, 1953, Major General Earle

Standlee was appointed Chief Surgeon of the United States Army Far East.

The date of my uncle's appointment to run the U.S. military and medical facilities at Camp Zama, twenty-five miles southwest of Tokyo, was certainly no accident. The Korean War, also known as a "police action" by authority of the United Nations, officially ended the very next day. For the next three years, Earle would redirect Camp Zama toward what President Kennedy later called "a hard and bitter peace," knowing full well that Korea remained divided and taking in evacuees and refugees from that country the entire time he and my aunt were stationed in Japan.

Everybody thinks they know what Army medicine looked like during the Korean War, and that's no accident either. Working with medical men like Uncle Earle back in the States, the Army studied the challenges it (and he) had faced recently with fast-moving commanders like General Patton, and made a major change.

The Mobile Army Surgical Hospital was conceived by Michael E. DeBakey, later famous as a heart surgeon in Houston, and other surgical consultants. The idea was an alternative to the system of portable surgical hospitals, field hospitals and general hospitals used in combat, and it was designed to get experienced personnel closer to the front. Casualties were treated first at the point of injury, then routed through an aid station for emergency stabilizing surgery, and finally sent to the mobile unit for more extensive treatment. During the Korean War, history tells us, a seriously wounded soldier who made it to a mobile unit alive had a greater than ninety-seven percent chance of survival once he received treatment.

Of course, nobody in the Army called these facilities "Mobile Army Surgical Hospitals." As the world knows from a book, a movie and many years of TV shows, the military used only the acronym, MASH.

→ *Shrine in postwar Japan*

The Camp Zama my Uncle Earle ran beginning in 1953, and
that my mother and I visited, had many historical monuments
related to the *Rikugun Shikan Gakko*—the Japanese Imperial
Military Academy it had been—and its students. Sometimes
accurately described as Imperial Japan's West Point, the school was
a major force in turning out officers and other combatants during
the crucial period between September 1937 and August 1945. The
letters, diaries and journals written by these young men reveal a
generation focused on how they could best serve their country.
Expecting no return from the fighting, the nineteen- and twenty-
year-old men erected graduation monuments on the campus before
departing, as though they were erecting their own tombstones.

It didn't take us long visiting Camp Zama with Uncle Earle and
Aunt Mary to hear about Duke. Shortly after General Douglas
MacArthur stepped on Japanese soil at what is now Atsugi Naval
Air Station, the medics from the 128th Station Hospital and
the Military Police arrived in this area to assist in the release of
American prisoners of war. Setting up the 1st Medical Installation

at Camp Zama, the commanding officer of the 128th arrived at the Japanese Military Hospital, Sagami-Ono, to accept its surrender on September 26, 1945. Only General Kiyoshi Shimazu, Japanese commanding general of the hospital, and his white horse awaited his arrival. In the traditional manner, the Japanese commander surrendered his sword. He also surrendered his horse, which the Americans setting up Camp Zama quickly christened Duke.

Originally owned by the Japanese Imperial family, Duke was adopted as mascot of the hospital, and probably hauled more soldiers on his back than any horse in the Far East. Later, when the hospital was to know another influx of wounded men from Korea, Duke was an important part of the therapy department, ridden by many of the wounded GIs. Finally, he had the misfortune of stepping into a hole and breaking his leg.

The horse was ordered destroyed, yet after considerable pleading from Duke's Japanese groom, his life was spared and he was nursed back to health. Duke spent his declining years donating blood for American research at the 406th Medical General Laboratory. He died of old age in August 1957 and is buried on the Camp Zama grounds.

As Earle and Mary's single surviving child, Wanda Buechler of Wichita Falls, describes it, the period spent in Japan was probably the most important in her parents' lives. It's noteworthy that Wanda's four children knew their grandparents only *after* their return to Texas—but instead of "Grandpa and Grandma," they always called Earle and Mary Papa-san and Mama-san.

My uncle's last official act as a military doctor came after his retirement from the Army as a two-star general in 1957. Commuting from Dallas to Chicago to work with the American Medical Association, he was asked to head up planning of a medical response to a successful nuclear attack on U.S. soil. In a sense, he was assigned to design medical care for a bomb several times more powerful than the ones my father had worked on in Oak Ridge, theoretically exploded by the Soviet Union in the heart of a major American population center.

It was the Cold War, of course. Working under authority from the Civil Defense Act of 1950, and with knowledge of the hydrogen bomb successfully detonated in November 1950 and the uranium bomb set off in February and March 1954, Earle and his time set about planning what to do medically about more than a million casualties on U.S. soil.

"With the advent of the larger weapons and the knowledge of their vastly increased destructive capabilities," my uncle wrote in the AMA's Special Study Project Report, "civil defense began to take on a newer meaning: national survival with the capability of the surviving population to arise from the ashes of mass destruction and piece together the remaining segments of national economy to support the armed forces in waging war to a successful conclusion."

As Uncle Earle put his team—teams, really, since the project divided its personnel into several key areas of study—through their undeniably grim paces, they settled on a location to use for planning, the Twin Cities of Minneapolis and St. Paul. As Earle explained in the group's report, published in January 1959, the cities were on a Civil Defense list of critical targets for nuclear attack, and indeed both could be destroyed by a single twenty-megaton ground burst. There were other factors that intrigued the group as well, from the proximity of the Mississippi River and its surrounding forests to the nearby Mayo Clinic, with its 800 physicians and a bed count that could be expanded quickly to 9,200. Earle also lauded Minnesota for having state Civil Defense legislation in place that would provide "strict discipline" in the event of nuclear medical emergency.

In a way similar to the method my father always used to plan, contract and build highways, Uncle Earle's report considers all the variables and sets out a basic structure to deal with them.

Of course, we should all be grateful that this structure was never needed, in Minneapolis-St. Paul or anywhere else in the United States. But it's clear that the U.S. military and its civilian authorities, faced with a prospect almost beyond imagining, turned to perhaps its greatest military-medical light to imagine it anyway.

"At no time in history has such a challenge been presented to any professional organization as that currently posed on medicine by the threat of an all-out war involving the continental United States," Earle wrote. "Not only is it the duty of organized medicine but it is the right and privilege of physicians in the United States, through the AMA, to assume the lead in advising the government on plans for both preventative and curative medicine to be implemented in case of national disaster."

→ *Japanese scene after the war*

As it turned out, my Aunt Mary also did some writing that earned a place in the history of military medicine—though it seemed to elude any form of publication until after her death in Texas in 1985. As early as 1938, Mary started collecting anecdotes about the history of Walter Reed Army Medical Center, where both she and Uncle Earle were working at the time. Since she stayed on at Walter Reed, through World War II and into the early 1950s, she had plenty of time to collect anecdotes and finally begin to organize them into a manuscript of 399 pages with about 300 historical photographs.

Somewhere along the way, the project took on the title *Borden's Dream*, a tribute to Lieutenant Colonel William Cline Borden, the most important man in the facility's founding—even though he lobbied successfully to name the place after a close friend, the Army physician who confirmed that yellow fever was transmitted by mosquitoes. Despite appreciative comments all around, the surprisingly personal and even chatty history of Walter Reed's first forty years, filled with observations of everyday life, never found its way into print during Mary's lifetime.

Borden's Dream finally did see the light of day in 2009, appearing a quarter century after its author's death and more than twenty years after my uncle passed away as well. Because of the narrative's length and style, the publishing Borden Institute held many discussions on how much or how little to edit. In the end, they decided to follow Aunt Mary's own guidance, given during one of the book's two near-misses. "I would not want anyone to update it to carry through later administrations," she'd written. "It represents the end of an era...It is a 'period piece' and not Swedish Modern. Let's keep it that way."

➤ *Mary Standlee*

No irony involved in all these decades of collecting and writing, of course, could equal the irony of the book's long-awaited publication. Aunt Mary's beloved "period piece" about Walter Reed appeared just as the nation's most famous military hospital was being shut down.

THE WORLD
Awaits

CHAPTER EIGHT

Sometimes, the most dramatic events of your life are ushered in with the least dramatic, or in fact most bureaucratic, of language. "Motor vehicles are influencing more and more the national economy of all nations," observes the Egyptian Highway Study, three years before its primary author hired my father away from the Texas Highway Department and sent him to Egypt, thus thrusting him, my mother and me into the greatest danger of our lives.

→ *Ships in Suez Canal*

Still, the study's calm continues, oblivious to all that historians would later call the Suez Crisis. "If roads are to be an asset, they must provide the most direct course feasible between all parts of the country, and they must be constructed so as to remain smooth and firm with a minimum of maintenance. Unfortunately many roads in Egypt simply follow the canals."

I suppose it was inevitable. In addition to my father's terrific Texas Highway Department record, he had worked within the military establishment during a world war and also spent time with that private construction company in Dallas. As the globe slowly rose from its wartime ashes, as countries rebuilt with dollars from the Marshall Plan and as America started competing for hearts and minds with the Soviets in the Cold War, my father's skill set was perfect for a visionary like Charles M. Upham.

As we've seen, Upham had been preaching the gospel according to highways in the United States since the end of World War I. With the end of World War II, his potential congregation was looking to get a whole lot bigger.

Filling in the blanks a little: my father assisted the Egyptian government, then under the control of Gamal Abdel Nasser, another in a long line of Cold War dictators who seemed like America's friend against the Soviet menace until they seemed more like our enemy. My father worked with the Roads and Bridges Department the entire time he was in Egypt, assisting and advising on a long series of projects that began with the crucial expressway connecting the capital of Cairo on the Nile and the ancient city of Alexandria on the Mediterranean. Daddy could not know how crucial that expressway would prove to be, since it delivered his family from the former to the latter in 1956, when war broke out pitting Egypt against Israel and the waning colonial powers of England and France. Other tasks that made it into my father's notes include preparing a construction manual that was specific to Egypt and assisting in lectures given at the government's training center in Cairo.

Every job Elmer Calvin would undertake for Charles M. Upham after that, until he retired as a company vice-president, would cover much of the same ground—and face many of the same challenges. Assist, advise, train, lecture, create, coordinate— these are words that resonate through Daddy's yellowed resume, every bit as much as words like Tegucigalpa or Bangkok. Still, the Egypt posting was the first and, happily, last time the world staged an actual war that we as a family were forced to flee.

As one of three construction engineers on the project, my father was invited to join Upham himself in Cairo, where he flew via Dallas and New York and then a night in Paris. Nonstop flights to anywhere were rare in those days, and few people would turn down a night in Paris. From there it was southeast across the Mediterranean to Cairo, where he joined the boss along with a woman known as Miss Wynne (an attorney and associate of the firm); Stanley Williamson, former State Highway Engineer of North Carolina, and a mechanical engineer from Florida.

Upon arrival, the company put my father up at Moreland House, a boarding house owned by a British woman who had married an Egyptian. Sadly, my father remembered years later, she cooked more in the style of England than of Egypt. The idea was that he'd stay at the boarding house until my mother and I joined him a few weeks later. We too ended up living at Moreland House for a time.

For all the danger and fear surrounding our exodus from Egypt, I loved the time we spent there. I got to watch my father go to and come home from work as an engineer in the ancient land that had virtually invented engineering. Not long after arriving in Egypt I got to see the pyramids, which at the time were on the outskirts of Cairo. I was happy during our months in Egypt, and I felt completely safe. As a teenaged girl on her first adventure in a very strange country, I don't remember ever feeling harassed or threatened on the streets of Cairo. I remember leaving the flat we ended up renting, pressing my way through noisy throngs of donkeys, camels and carts where in America the cars would certainly be, but never once feeling danger. People tell me that wouldn't necessarily be the case in Egypt today.

Nothing quite prepares you for Cairo, not even living there. You're still not prepared for the first time you go to the old train station, where mobs pushing to get out smash into mobs pushing to get in, and where every traveler seems to carry a tattered suitcase and a plywood crate holding a chicken or a goat. You're still not prepared for the call to worship, echoes from minarets all over the city, five times each day. And you're still not prepared for that moment your choice of quiet, closely pressed-in street opens into a broad, leafy square, with only the hot blue sky above and what seems like the entire earth's population below. Every piece of ground that ought to hold one person is holding two or three, plus taxis and trucks moving through with a heavy hand on the horn, plus camels and donkeys dragging carts with tingling bells. All that, and the engine exhaust and the dust from the desert and the meat-pungent cooking smoke, and the shouting.

That was Tahrir, or Liberation Square in 1956, though I couldn't begin to read its name in the graceful squiggles of Arabic that filled every street sign. All I knew was that this was home to the legendary Egyptian Museum, where any young American's dreams of hieroglyphics and mummies could be right before your eyes. Imagine my emotions, seeing that same square on television more than fifty years later, the center of Egypt's Arab Spring revolution.

In Egypt, for the first time, but hardly for the last, my parents entered the social whirl that spread out from the American Embassy to embrace the most distinguished of foreign diplomats and businessmen as well as the wealthiest of locals. It was a heady life, perhaps for my parents as well, but definitely for me at fifteen. I have so many memories of wonderful times during those too-brief months we spent in Egypt, a fact that surely contributes even now to my overall fondness for the country and its people.

I remember, for instance, going to horse races and polo matches at the Gezira Sporting Club, founded in 1882 and leased to the exclusive province of the British military, and dressing up like all the other ladies in high heels and a straw hat. That was usually on Sundays, with other socializing via swimming and tennis at the Maadi Sporting Club. Still other days my friends and I would go to movies—in huge, once-glorious opera houses

→ *Scene in Mouski*

→ *Elmer's days in Cairo*

now reduced by changing times to running film through clicking projectors. We'd be sure to stop for ice cream at a shop called Groppi on the way home. I remember shopping trips with Mother to the tangle of narrow walkways in Mouski, buying lovely brass pieces and leather goods at a real bargain, and enjoying the sight of Egyptian men sitting and smoking their water pipes called *shisha*. And I remember parties under tents at the edge of town by the pyramids. I don't remember the temperatures being painfully high—but then again, we were always under those tents, with that strange, whirring music playing and belly dancers swirling among us.

As a practical matter, we lived in the dusty, crowded center of Cairo near the U.S. Embassy, the Shepherd Hotel and the Nile—which would prove a godsend when we were ordered to gather at the embassy for our immediate rescue. The Americans working in Cairo had a school, the Cairo American College, in a small town called Maadi up the Nile. It didn't take my mother long to get hired there, teaching second grade. And it didn't take me long to get registered there at the high school. Mother and I traveled from Cairo each day, and as with most things in our life in Egypt, that was a "local color" experience to be remembered.

Despite the demands of his work, my father also tried hard to help Mother and me do tourist things during the early weeks we were in Cairo. I remember our days there as carefree but, looking back, there was more than enough going on that my father might have sensed something, might have decided we should do the must-see checklist sooner rather than later. One of my memories includes a barbecue on the beach east of Alexandria, which featured an admiral in the Egyptian Navy telling a story about his English and French counterparts. It came from a time when the British and French were enemies, and it featured the legendary Admiral Nelson.

"A French ship was being followed by a British ship commanded by Admiral Nelson along these shores," the Egyptian told us, nodding out past the waves crawling up onto the brown sand. "The French ship pulled in for the night down there where our port is now. The British ship followed, turned sails and moved out to sea. The French crew drew a sigh of relief and relaxed. However, as you know, each evening about dark, the wind changes, and a gentle cool breeze blows from north to south. Between midnight and 1 a.m. the British ship floated gently beside the French ship, and the British sailors jumped aboard with their swords drawn. The entire French crew jumped overboard and never returned."

On another excursion that my father arranged, we visited what would prove to be the dispute at the heart of the Suez Crisis—the Canal that opened in 1869 after ten years of construction. There was, apparently, no road from El Mansoura, where he was doing some reconnaissance, to Port Said at the Mediterranean mouth of the canal, which funneled international shipping south to the Red Sea. He had my mother and me catch a bus to El Mansoura and hired a driver to take the three of us to tour the canal. Since there was no road, my father researched high and low tides so we could be driven the entire way along the beach. We headed out during low tide at 5 a.m., arriving at Port Said right before high tide came in about six hours later.

It was quite an engineer's tour of a great world landmark of engineering, similar to a visit to the Panama Canal. Picking up a 35 mm camera to shoot slides (my father said he took thousands over the next sixteen years), we drove down the west side of the canal to the point it emptied into the Red Sea, visited and took pictures of everything we could, and then headed back to Cairo along a fairly good road. One of the images my father never forgot was a life-size statue of the British engineer who designed the Canal. "Later that fall," my father recalled, "his statue was blasted to pieces."

→ *Our flat in Cairo's Garden City*

Whatever my father believed that day about what was going to happen, as a teenager at the time I can certainly say I had no idea.

There are several entire books in any library about the Suez Crisis that shook up the entire world in October and November of 1956. It certainly shook up (and abruptly ended) our idyllic life with my father in Egypt. While we were touring the pyramids and the wonders of the Egyptian Museum, large powers were at work on large plans, most of them without their citizens knowing.

At first, for instance, the U.S. and several other European countries agreed to finance Nasser's dream of a high dam on the Nile at Aswan, but then they backed out suddenly when they learned the Egyptian dictator was taking loan offers from the Soviets as well. In response to this rebuff by the West, a fuming Nasser took over the Suez Canal to nationalize it (years before that was contractually supposed to happen) and announced he would use revenues from the ships passing through to build his dam. There were many sabers rattled between the Egyptians, the British and the French—all three countries with big stakes in the Canal—as well as within Israel, which had and still has a big stake in anything that changes the Arab World.

As my family enjoyed the sunny October weather along the Nile, the three parties excluded by the Egyptian decision came to a secret agreement, something that historians now call "collusion" and "conspiracy." Israel would invade Egypt with an attack across the Sinai, then England and France would issue a ceasefire ultimatum to both sides. Certain that no one would stop fighting, England and France would then attack Egypt too, taking back the Suez Canal.

The deal for Egypt was so bad and, allowed Israel to keep so much territory that one angry British diplomat later characterized it this way: "The burglar, having been caught in the act of breaking and entering, had been told by the two policemen who found him to take half the contents of the safe, while they moved in to take the rest."

As President Eisenhower had been dubious of any such invasion ideas—Ike considered the whole business "colonialism" by two

↳ *Elmer at the pyramids with guide/translator*

waning Old World powers, and he hated colonialism—the three didn't even mention to the U.S. that any of this was happening. They simply evacuated their civilians. Therefore, in Cairo, the U.S. didn't mention it to us either, until my parents and I had to flee.

Israeli paratroopers were dropped deep in the Sinai Desert, launching full-scale war with Egypt on October 29. The very next day, word reached us from the State Department that all Americans were to gather at the U.S. Embassy on October 31 to make our way to Alexandria. By the time we were all assembling at the embassy, British and French planes began their attack, dropping bombs on Egyptian defenses all over Cairo. For the first time in my young life, jets streaking overhead, bombs exploding miles or merely blocks away and the rat-tat-tat of anti-aircraft weaponry became part of my personal soundtrack. For what I think was the first time in my life, I realized that my father, my mother and I could be killed.

What followed was a nightmare. At some point, while still at the embassy, my father told my mother and me that he would escort us to the rescue ships in Alexandria but then needed to join Mr. Upham returning to Cairo. For one thing, he said, there were still business issues that had to be finalized, and for another there was the $250.00 deposit he'd put down on our apartment. All these years later, with so many world powers trying to blow each other up all around us, that seems such an insignificant amount of money. My mother and I were upset by my father's decision, since we wished all of us could be safe together far from bombs. Yet in some way we must have understood.

Starting out, we were thirty-one cars in an American convoy, heading north along the Cairo-Alexandria highway that my father had been brought here to improve. Packed into our car, everytime we looked at a window in any direction, we saw explosions and the fires they left behind, along with the flickering flashes of distant artillery. Locals, of course, were not out for a drive, but the going was impossibly slow. We were stopped by Egyptian military many times, grilling our leaders, thumbing through our papers. We didn't know if we should be afraid of them. Our country was not attacking Egypt. But we couldn't be sure the men with the guns knew that.

After hours and hours of tense stop-and-go, we pulled into the ancient city of Alexandria and started making our way toward the port. Being strategic, there was even more bombing here than in Cairo. I'm sure many of us wondered if we'd made our way this far only to be killed when a bomb fell on our car.

My parents tried to comfort me, but as I noticed each time we'd gathered along the route, tension among the Americans was moving toward hysteria. We were not soldiers, trained to deal with situations like this. We were American diplomats, their wives and children, some cars packed to the rafters with baby strollers and stuffed animals, grabbed up in the frenzy of emergency departure. Many women and children were crying by the time we, as a group, were waved by Egyptian soldiers onto the freight-packed Alexandria docks. Still, the American rescue boats were not yet allowed to leave, so we spent the night near the port at the Beau Rivage Hotel.

None of us who escaped by sea the next day will ever forget the happiest sight of all: a harbor with several gray Navy warships flying the red, white and blue, plus a cluster of U.S. Marines gathered around a landing craft with its mouth wide open to carry us out of fear. The Marines were under Egyptian orders to carry no weapons, so it was the mere sight of their uniforms, and the smiles they gave us as they hoisted women and children from the concrete onto the rocking vessel that made us think our ordeal was winding down.

Our group, waiting to head out to the ships, was already what it would be for the next several days: a nest of rumors. The harbor was blocked; the harbor was not blocked. The harbor

→ *Convoy forms at American Embassy*

was mined; the harbor was not mined. All I could do was kiss my father goodbye—forever?—and let my mother take me into her arms as the landing craft pulled away from the dock and made its way through floating destruction to our ship.

I think we were taken to the *U.S.S. Chilton*, though there were two other American warships "waging peace" in Alexandria that day, the *Fort Snelling* and the *Thuban*. We didn't realize it at the time, but there were other U.S. Navy ships, all belonging to the 6th Fleet, rescuing Americans from Haifa on the coast of Israel as well. We all felt the engines throbbing up beneath us and through us and then noticed the shoreline moving only because we were, and then we watched as our ship and its brethren passed out of the harbor and into the beginnings of open sea. I'm sure some of us cheered. Others chose to simply remember the Egyptian soldiers at the machine gun posts, waving to us wildly and grinning. They at least understood that we weren't the enemy.

"Outside."

That's the communication I now know was sent from our lead ship to 6th Fleet headquarters, prompting a response that was clearly deserved by our sailors and Marines alike: "Your one-word

→ *Evacuation from the port of Alexandria*

message is a classic. Your successful evacuation of over 1,500 without fuss or feathers is an outstanding accomplishment." Fuss or feathers? The man saying that hadn't had to make his way from Cairo by car on the "expressway" Daddy hadn't had the opportunity to build.

At sea, the Navy went out of its way to make us all feel at home. While I do remember spending time under blankets on deck, it's also true that officers aboard the *Chilton, Fort Snelling* and *Thuban* gave up their cabins so women and children could sleep indoors. I also was told about sailors cutting up cloth to make diapers for babies and breaking up wooden furniture to piece together cribs and playpens.

One baby was even born on the *Chilton* as we steamed away from Egypt, watching the brown silt from the Nile finally let go and give us Homer's "wine-dark sea." I don't remember what that little boy's family name was. But his parents decided his first name had to be "Chilton." The Navy later gave the new parents a plaque on the "launching," with the "fond wish that his journey through life may be accompanied by fair winds and following seas."

Because we weren't sailors any more than we were soldiers, we were a bit vulnerable to rumors about where they were taking us and why. There was much talk of Beirut, for example, and I really thought we were heading there, but then there was talk that Lebanon had refused to let us land. Other people repeated different rumors, adults talking in fear and chaos—even as the young children seemed calmer. Many of these were dubbed "junior Marines" and given carbines without any ammunition to march and grill around the deck.

This kept them busy and active, with their minds far from their problems. I remember one sailor talking about a group of eight- to twelve-year-olds who "grew into a close-knit group with an *esprit de corps* that challenged that of the U.S. Marine Corps itself." Maybe those kids' parents should have been made to do the same.

It was days, but felt like weeks, that we were at sea—probably a testament to how much we all longed to feel we were someplace safe. And for most of us, that meant not only protected by the mighty U.S. 6th Fleet but standing on solid ground. Solid ground, however, was still at least one more ship away. We were taken to a place called Souda Bay on the large Greek island of Crete and, with no adequate docking facilities available, transferred in groups by landing craft to a mammoth troop carrier called the *S.S. Patch*.

This at least meant more cabins and hammocks for all of us, though the time it took for all of us to get there and join our countrymen rescued from Haifa dragged things out even more. In addition, we had to take on food and water in Souda Bay, since nothing in anybody's strategic plans called for what was now 2,000 or so extra passengers.

Before heading back to Cairo, my father had promised we'd be together again in Rome or someplace close to it—a fact that tells me he knew more about the evacuation plans than most of the people being evacuated. Then again, working alongside Charles M. Upham put him very close to a wide variety of informed sources in the U.S. military and diplomatic corps. We were taken to the port of Naples, right there in that beautiful blue bay in the shadow of Mt. Vesuvius, the now gentle-looking slope that had long ago destroyed Pompeii.

We've all seen the tradition of bending to kiss the ground of countries when you arrive. I was never more tempted than I was that day, going ashore from the *Patch* onto the solid ground of NATO-member Italy.

Being my father and working for the ever-connected Mr. Upham with his omnipresent Miss Wynne, Daddy ended up having quite an adventure as well. All we have is his narrative set to paper some years after the fact. Riding with Mr. Upham, he returned to Cairo and went straight to the airport in hopes of arranging some kind of flight. Mr. Upham knew the Cairo manager for American Airlines, who told him the company's thirty personnel were on standby but probably not flying anywhere soon.

As though to confirm that analysis, British planes chose that moment to open up on the airport with bombs and machine guns, and of course the Egyptians started firing back. My father recalled being stopped by an Egyptian military police officer, who advised Mr. Upham to keep his U.S. passport close at hand. "You look like a Frenchman," the officer said with a smile, "and you talk like an Englishman." I guess he felt my father from Texas did neither.

My father did manage to get back his almighty $250.00 deposit when he got back "home" that evening. Then, near 8 p.m., the British bombing of Cairo resumed, with my father able to look out at the scene from our flat's window. "The bomber droned on," he recalled, "at a reported elevation of about 40,000 feet and the anti-aircraft fire exploded heavily below. Soon I heard explosions in the direction of Maadi. We became restless to leave and bought train tickets to Khartoum, we then would fly to Rome. That evening the British announced that their next target would be all rail facilities. We lost our train ticket money."

Finally, I'm sure with much Upham urging, the airline manager arranged a flight out to Rome—from an airport in Libya 240 kilometers west along the cost. Transport was arranged: a car for Upham, Miss Wynne and Daddy, a pickup truck for baggage, gasoline and drinking water. Leaving from Alexandria early in the morning, my father asked the driver to turn around for a moment, so he could take one last look at the skies above the ancient city in the ancient land of Egypt. The driver agreed, then pointed the car west across the deserts.

My father remembered, shortly after they crossed the border into Libya, spotting some of the largest oil-drilling equipment he'd ever seen, even after spending most of his life in Texas. He seemed to take comfort in being told that it belonged to the Hunt Oil Co. of Dallas. They spent the night near the airport with only one vacant room, Miss Wynne taking that, my father and his boss draping themselves over chairs in the lobby.

The morning finally came, then breakfast, and then the airport. In the one moment that my father's exodus from Egypt most resembled ours, he wrote down later: "I was certainly glad to see that American plane waiting to take us to Rome." After joining Mother and me in the Italian capital, we headed home. But Daddy did so by way of a visit with Uncle Earle in Japan.

Historians have had much to say about the Suez Crisis of 1956, which ended quickly with a ceasefire sought by our country, since everone could see where the political winds were blowing. For one thing, the mishandling of the invasion toppled the governments of two of our traditional allies, tossing out Anthony Eden in England and Guy Mollet in France. The French took the debacle especially hard, coming on the heels of their traumatic defeat in Indochina. They'd turn to Charles de Gaulle, the World War II hero of the French Resistance, as their leader and work to be proud of being French again.

In Egypt, far from being toppled from power, Nasser actually gained in strength. He was not the first, and definitely not the last, Arab leader to become larger-than-life by demonizing Israel and the West, both of whom may for once have deserved it.

And Eisenhower? Well, all the time the Suez Crisis was going on, he was also keeping a close eye on his chosen enemy, the Soviets, who were invading Hungary to crush a courageous flourish of freedom there. Turns out, they were too busy to get involved in Egypt after all. And all that time, Eisenhower was also running for a second term. In America, it was politics as usual. Ike defeated Adlai Stevenson by a healthy margin (while my mother and I were at sea) and ran the country pretty successfully for another four years.

He replaced the so-called Truman Doctrine of confronting communism wherever it raised its ugly head with a policy of, well, confronting communism wherever it raised its ugly head. They called it the Eisenhower Doctrine. In fact, with his Cold War mindset, Ike found himself dealing more and more with that formerly French Indochina—which we would all get to know a lot better soon, by a different name: Vietnam.

➔ *Carolyn during evacuation, wearing Marine's helmet*

That was still in the future, though. So, Ike referred to the Suez Crisis, not the Vietnam War, when he said: "I just don't know what got into those people. It's the damnedest business I ever saw supposedly intelligent governments get themselves into."

OVERSEAS *Highways*

CHAPTER NINE

After our family's close call in Egypt, requiring the 6th Fleet, the grace of God and Charles M. Upham to get us out, my father might well have returned to our home on Beverly Drive in Dallas to live out his life in peace.

As he related it in old age, people were asking him when he was going to retire even before he took us to Egypt. Yet that route, I now see, would not suffice for my father. Beginning in the Central American country of Honduras and continuing another eighteen years until he actually did retire after working in Kuwait, Daddy was many things to many people. The one thing most of us didn't realize—until now, in fact, years after his death—was that he was, first and foremost, a Cold Warrior.

Maybe you wouldn't think that today, after words like *détente* and *perestroika* enjoyed their day in the political sun, indeed after the fall of the Soviet Union and the liberation of the entire Eastern Bloc. But my father's resume was assembled during the Cold War's prime time. Looking back, the same Elmer Calvin who had played a notable role at Oak Ridge in winning World War II devoted the rest of his working life to winning a far less defined but, to its combatants, no less deadly war.

In 1945, after the Japanese surrender, the larger world entered a brief period of hope and idealism—the United Nations was born of such feelings, as well as the far more controversial notion that the "nuclear secrets" General Groves and others had kept so long should be shared with our wartime allies, including Stalin's Soviet Union. Behind the scenes, however, all sides were already not only distrusting each other but expecting that a third world war pitting the United States against the Soviet Union would follow. Some, especially within the military, even hoped it would happen soon, before all the American soldiers had gotten comfortable back in civilian life. It didn't fall out that way, for a lot of reasons, despite warnings from American generals like Patton and MacArthur. Of course, combat generals never do understand peacetime very well.

Two U.S. military leaders, however, emerged from the war with major peacetimes ahead of them—Eisenhower to move into the White House in 1952 and, more directly setting the stage for my father's work, George Marshall to take up rebuilding Germany, Japan and the rest of the battered world. What came to be known as the Marshall Plan was viewed with lots of hindsight as the perfect blend of early Cold War generosity and self-protectiveness. Anywhere on earth the United States could rebuild, the thinking went at the time, we would rebuild in our own image, a fertile ground for the democracy and, yes, the capitalism that the Soviets always vowed to overwhelm.

The Marshall Plan's humanitarian thrust was altogether real, born of a great nation's compassion even for those it had been forced to vanquish. But to see no self-interest in all we did after the war is to be naïve, if not to question why we did so much at all.

My father's labors to build highways in foreign countries after Egypt reflected the lingering presumptions of the Marshall Plan, that the United States as leader of the free world had an obligation to bring those less fortunate into the light of modernity and progress. Yet it also reflected the other side of the 1950s coin, the one typically ascribed to the Truman Doctrine. Rather than

→ *Road grading in Honduras*

prepare for all-out nuclear conflagration with the Soviet Union, something families of that time certainly feared, the doctrine projected an endless flurry of small conflagrations, some in countries in remote parts of the world that many Americans had never heard of. Each time trouble broke out between two parties within such a country, it was assumed that we would back one side and the Russians would back the other. And with that, even if World War III could be avoided, the world's future hung in the balance.

Following so close upon our time in Egypt, Honduras could not have been more different—something that, even as a teenager, I had to notice as my mother arranged to teach at the American school there and I arranged to take high school classes. Instead of endless stretches of yellow-brown desert the minute you moved away from the green banks of the Nile, Honduras seemed one big, bright green jungle. I thought it was all lovely, especially after Egypt. And instead of hot, dry desert air there was hot, wet jungle air, with seldom more than a few hours between brief assaults of rain. Welcome to the tropics, I thought. Welcome to a banana republic that grows real bananas.

My father's task in Honduras was huge and seemingly opened-ended, though of course Charles M. Upham wouldn't have agreed to a project without set parameters. Still, the notion of surveying nearly all the significant roads and bridges in a country pressed between Nicaragua, El Salvador, Guatemala and the Caribbean Sea, taking note of their conditions and starting the process of fixing the problems, struck me as being mammoth. Maybe it had always been this way in my father's work, and I was finally getting old enough to understand.

During our early days in Honduras, according to the project notes, Daddy and his team made field trips from San Pedro Sula across the Chamelecon Bridge to La Lima, from San Pedro Sula to Puerto Cortés, along the West Road to Santa Rosa de Copán, and finally along roads leading into the capital of Tegucigalpa. They also checked out river crossings by ferry and at least one railway bridge.

In retrospect, what they found in Honduras was probably what they were expecting: poorly planned, poorly routed roads that were poorly constructed and even more poorly maintained. At spots along various routes, tractors, bulldozers and other pieces of heavy equipment sat idle, nonfunctional really, valuable only when some other equipment needed a spare part. And the department in charge of all this, simply called *Caminos*, was a disorganized mess, with very confusing chains of command, almost zero budget control and reporting, and no particular training for employees new or old.

"The general maintenance of the road surface was in deplorable condition," my father wrote as Upham's lead engineer. "This was obviously a condition which any average maintenance patrol would correct. It indicated the complete lack of patrol, or a complete lack of interest in the safety of the driving public."

I'm looking now at an almost-nostalgic blast from the past: the detailed, 100-plus-page report my father prepared, with page after page of yellowed, black-and-white snapshots applied to pages with glue that has long since ceased to hold. Photo after photo shows roads—some in a charming "before and after" format, plus hundreds of pieces of equipment that don't seem capable of doing anything or going anywhere. The report makes a lengthy series of recommendations and comments on each of the roads visited, ranging from what needs to be done to the proper materials needed to do it. One of the photos even shows a Honduran government official addressing a small crowd gathered for an opening ceremony, proving that at least some of these improvements were completed during the time we spent in the country.

A modern inquiring mind might want to know: What was a respected professional like Elmer Calvin doing in a small, presumably not-very-strategic place like Honduras?

Honduras was a textbook banana republic. Indeed, one of its major money crops, since the beginning of the 20th century, had always been bananas. Thanks to the workings of a company called United Fruit, these bananas made their way out of the Honduran jungle to be loaded onto steamers headed for, more often than not, the port of New Orleans. In addition to there being a market in the U.S. for bananas and a few other "tropical fruits," United Fruit succeeded in Honduras and other Central American countries because of two things. It kept the cost of hiring laborers low, thus resisting any efforts to unionize, organize or even encourage the notion of workers having rights. And it did so by supporting, financially first and most importantly, a series of mostly military dictatorships that handled the local dirty work.

The dictator of Honduras during my father's time building

roads there was Ramón Villeda Morales, who in those years had to fend off two separate coups and fight off military actions along its border with Nicaragua. With the help of U.S. State Department documents, however, it's clear that the revolt that mattered was in neither of those countries but on an island across the Caribbean.

Fidel Castro was busy establishing a revolutionary and eventually Soviet-aligned communist regime only about ninety miles from the tip of Florida. The earlier communist takeover of China had frightened nearly every American; but China was a lot farther away than the Key West where Truman himself kept his second White House.

> "Villeda was clearly perceived," wrote the State Department in its internal summary of my father's time in Honduras, "as someone friendly to the United States and aware of the dangers of international communism. From this perspective, it was not surprising that... the Department of State took extraordinary measures to arrange loans for the financially troubled United Fruit Company, since it was felt that collapse by the company would seriously destabilize the Honduran economy, cause loss of jobs, threaten the future of the Villeda administration, provide a seed bed for communist discontent, and deprive local Honduran communities of numerous public services which United Fruit provided in the absence of the Honduran Government's ability to do so."

Elmer Calvin's time working out of the Honduran capital of Tegucigalpa coincided with revolts against this U.S.-backed

President, as well as with Castro's successful overthrow of the U.S.-backed Batista Regime in Cuba. We know now that many in Washington feared the same sort of revolution in Honduras and other Central American countries. The efforts of our CIA to remove or even assassinate Castro were not merely intended to return democracy to one Caribbean island but to remove the inspiration of having a communist model so nearby. Creating a stable-looking Villeda government that could be seen building new roads and highways, connecting farms and villages in the same way my father had done in rural Texas, seemed one of the best ways to confront our enemies in the Cold War.

The single event I remember best from that time concerned the visit of Richard M. Nixon, then vice-president serving under Eisenhower and one hundred percent the Cold Warrior until much later in his political career. Though only a "goodwill visit" to several Central American countries that figured in our efforts to "contain" communism, I remember seeing Nixon and his daughter Tricia at several functions held in their honor by the Honduran government, first at the U.S. Embassy and later that

→ *Supervising the work*

day at the Tegucigalpa Country Club.

One Honduran writer, Roberto C. Ordóñez, remembers Nixon's visit to Tegucigalpa even better than I do, describing all the pretty young girls lining the route in colorful native dress, the throwing of kisses and tropical flowers and the efforts made beforehand to improve the roads and city streets over which the Nixons traveled. "Fifty years later," Ordóñez wrote in 2005, "the street is much worse, broken down, awaiting another president or important visitor, like Vice President Nixon."

My father was Upham's project manager, supervising the "assist and advise" portion of the company's contract with the Honduran government. As such, according to his resume, he provided a "multi-faceted program of maintenance of highways and equipment, procurement of equipment, location surveys and construction plans." It seems now a strange substitute for the rifles and artillery of World War II, and especially for the atomic, and later hydrogen, bombs in the U.S. arsenal. But in those years, aid became a new kind of weapon in a new kind of war.

It became such a powerful weapon that as soon as my father's work in Honduras let him and my mother think about returning to Dallas, Upham took him away from his family on the most secretive mission of his entire post-Manhattan Project career.

I was a teenager at the time, and I knew Mother was doing her best to make my father's absence seem like "business as usual." But when you don't hear from your father for almost six months, and when you know only that he's someplace on the other side of the world called Iran, there is no way not to.

As usual, my father's resume says little beyond the typical administrative platitudes. With Charles M. Upham and fellow engineer Stan Williamson, he made his way into Iran—which was under control of the Shah at that time, with several strategic similarities to President Villeda in Honduras—and then to a remote area southeast of Tehran called Kerman Province. Also as usual, his mission was to make the area less remote.

The engineers prepared an engineering and economic report on transportation in the Kerman area, covering not only the typical roads and highways but airports, railroads and ports. As presented to the Shah's government, this report pulled together "preliminary engineering estimates, priorities of construction and estimated amounts of equipment and personnel to initiate a complete highway program for this area."

As my father described his Iran assignment to me years later, the trip was an odd mix of frustrating work and almost as frustrating attempts at play. In this or most other centuries, a man may expect to visit Iran only once if at all, so anything you ever heard you might do there assembles itself into your itinerary. In addition to eating

→ *Highway in Kerman Province, Iran*

yogurt "better than we have," my father observed, Daddy spent his days assessing both forms of Iran's ground transportation, road and rail, with an eye not only for connecting Tehran to Kerman Province but possibly extending a future line to the coast. The study not only took my father along all roads between points A and B but up into the air as well, since Upham had decided to hire a plane and a pilot. Considering the vastness of the terrain, taking a bird's eye view of conditions made sense.

Daddy met dozens of Iranians during his half-year or so in their country, and all treated him with respect and even affection. Years later, he recalled visiting an oil strike there that reminded him of the fabled Spindletop near Beaumont back in Texas, ordering some roasted pistachios for his family back in Dallas after meeting a man who grew them, and visiting different places that baked bread and wove Persian carpets. He also traveled on his own to the Caspian Sea, where he saw the guard tower marking the border with the Soviet Union.

In the end, the Iran project was cut short when the Upham engineers recommended only a highway and not a rail line—and especially when, as my father understood it, a government representative asked for the hefty bribe required to remain in the government's good graces. "I knew that was coming," Upham told my father, once they were out of earshot.

Because my mother wasn't with him, I guess I imagined more than I actually knew about my father's time in Iran. It hardly rules out serving as "eyes and ears" for our government, but I found a letter much later that gives far greater detail. It was written, interestingly enough, to State Highway Engineer D.C. Greer back in Texas, care of the later-made-infamous U.S. Embassy in Tehran.

According to the single-spaced typed letter, Charles M. Upham was invited by a group calling themselves 'Electric Bond and Share Company' to form a group of consultants to conduct an economic survey, with Upham in charge of its transportation section. "As you know," my father wrote to Greer, "Iran has large oil revenues, and by proper legislation they formed an agency called *Plan Organization*, and the government has budgeted sixty percent of their oil revenues to their so-called 'Seven Year Plan' for the economic development of the country." Additionally, "The chances of our area developing into construction of any consequence will apparently be dependent upon the geologists of our group finding minerals in commercial qualities or the development of water resources for irrigation and power."

So there my father was, a man who had planned highways for Greer through places like Waxahachie in Texas, trying to explain to him highways through places like Kerman Province in Iran. If the main question here is "Why," the main answer lies again in the history of the Cold War.

Despite his tough-guy rise to power and his reliance on a vast and dreaded secret police known as SAVAK, the Shah of Iran had

→ *Aerial survey team in Iran*

been notable for his pro-Western, though not pro-democratic, stance since assuming the throne in 1952. A huge landmass filling the map between the Arab World that surrounded Israel along the shores of the Mediterranean and bordering the Soviet Union, Iran impressed itself upon U.S. officials at every turn. And that was before they even thought about all the oil the Shah could decide what to do with. Beginning with Eisenhower in the White House and running through presidents Kennedy, Johnson, Nixon, Ford and Carter, the United States would do just about anything it could think of to keep the Shah in power, even as intellectuals at home and abroad began the slow-bubbling revolution that would eventually drive the man into exile.

Internal State Department summaries of my father's six months in Kerman Province reflect a tense chapter in this process. Interestingly, U.S. diplomats then saw the SAVAK and other more official military branches as both the greatest defender *of* and the greatest threat *to* the Shah's stability on what was called the Peacock Throne. The country's financial difficulties, pushed along by terrible inflation, seemed the most likely source of unrest that the Shah's soldiers could choose to suppress or, in some scenarios, encourage.

This was 1959, not the eve of the Ayatollah's disastrous revolution in 1979, but the perceived Cold War and even post-Cold War dangers come through from our State Department's documents, loud and clear.

"There will be difficult periods in Iranian relations with the U.S. in the future, as there have been in the past," one report from my father's time states. "The Shah will seek more U.S. support and stronger guarantees of his security. At the same time he will attempt to reduce Soviet pressures on Iran. However, as long as the Shah remains dominant, we believe that the odds are against any significant change in Iran's basic Western orientation."

And another report has this to say, with more than a little prophecy:

> "While a political upheaval which resulted in removal of the Shah might lead to an anti-Western foreign policy, most of the top military leaders, as well as many of the moderate opposition civilian elements, would almost certainly continue to look to the West, particularly to the US, as a major source of protection for Iran. However, it is unlikely that any successor regime would take such an outspokenly pro-West stand as has the Shah."

For the United States, and arguably for the entire world, the forces that eventually drove the Shah from his throne—into exile and death from cancer—were not those pragmatic military leaders or even intellectual exiles troubled by the Shah's well-documented corruption and cruelty. They were religious fanatics unlikely to remember those six months that a man named Elmer

Calvin, representing the people of the United States, worked in Kerman Province to help an ancient, richly cultured and religiously tolerant area step forward into the 20th century. No one knew it then, but by the time Iranian "students" swarmed the U.S. Embassy taking hostages in 1979, the 20th century would catch the first train out of Iran.

Indochina

CHAPTER TEN

With hindsight, of course, it's easy to predict where my father's next assignment would be—though it seemed remote from anywhere important when he received it. For me now, it's clear what both the public and private purposes of my father's highway work actually were.

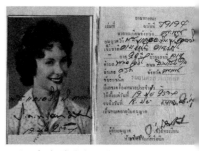

→ *Carolyn's Thai visa*

The time in Honduras: holding off the threat of Soviet communist revolution embodied by Castro's troublemaking in Cuba. The time in Iran: holding off the threat of Soviet communist revolution by propping up the Shah. After months spent out of touch in Iran, my father's next Upham assignment took him into the very heart of a new decade's darkness—the next chapter of the French debacle in the place they knew and cursed as *Indochine*.

The role of Thailand in the Vietnam Era is sometimes called the Secret War, and sometimes even the "Insignificant War." Yet the military and covert missions the United States and its Allies conducted against the communists of North Vietnam would often involve a beginning or an ending in Thailand, not to mention a significant number of volunteer troops from Thailand. You can imagine my surprise when I discovered that at least some of the loyalty of these volunteers was born during the exact years my father spent there and the exact work he was doing. In other words, imagine my surprise when I recognized my father's fingerprints on Thai history.

"The American-built roads that transformed rural Thailand's physical landscape and social and economic systems in the 1950s and 1960s also transformed its people," writes scholar Richard A. Ruth, describing a process that I might subtitle "The Good Roads Movement Goes to Thailand." "The infrastructure constructed with American aid, machinery, and advice profoundly altered the relationship between the people of the countryside and those of the urban center. For the first time in Thailand's history, the people and circumstances of the rural areas rivaled those of the capital in importance to the national state. The need for industrial labor, construction workers and service employees brought waves of internal migrants from what had once been Siam's hinterlands to live and work in Bangkok...And in doing so they changed Bangkok's self-image. These upcountry people redefined what it meant to be Thai."

The volunteer soldiers in Thailand, not to mention the U.S. military bases constructed there in the 1960s, spoke volumes about the layers of relationship created with my father's highways. The volunteers, many of whom came to the city from the country, fought while wearing American uniforms and carrying American weapons. They lived in American-built camps, using American currency to purchase American goods. They were treated for battlefield injuries in American hospitals. And some of their dead ended up buried on American soil. As Ruth expresses it, "In an age defined by an American idiom, they bore the marks of close contact with the Americans."

Despite considerable largesse moving in its direction from the United States—$650 million between 1950 and 1975 in economic aid, plus $940 million more for defense and security—the U.S. support was only secondarily mercenary. Most of it was strongly ideological, with Thais wanting to fight communism beyond their borders before it consumed their own land. In advocating violence, revolution and atheism, communism represented the antithesis of Thai cultural traditions.

In addition, the communist threat so recently materialized in Korea reminded Thais of their long-standing fears of conquest by the communist Chinese. Historically, ancient Siam had been a vassal to the Chinese Emperor, and the threat of Chinese domination was a very real part of Thai history. Most Thais believed it was the Chinese, not the Soviets at all, who were behind supposedly homegrown communist insurgencies throughout Southeast Asia. In other words, Thailand had, for a host of very different historical and cultural reasons, developed a Truman Doctrine of its own.

Still, taking such a public pro-American stance had its dangers. If, for instance, the United States did not prevail in Vietnam, Thailand could find itself all alone surrounded by communist neighbors—the ultimate victim of what U.S. politicians had lately started calling the "domino theory." Even more profoundly perhaps, the military alliance clearly would become a cultural one too, with the only Southeast Asian country to avoid European colonization in the 19th century backing into American "colonization" in the mid-20th. Only the fear of communist takeover, worst of all by the hated Chinese, convinced most Thais the bargain was a fair one.

Even if we postpone consideration of the military importance many of my father's highways would rather quickly take on, I can't overlook that his work in Thailand takes up nearly one and a half pages of his three-page resume. Partly, I think this is because the work was his most recent at the time of writing—his later efforts in Colombia, Bolivia, Turkey and Kuwait do not appear. Still, I'm sure that by the mid-1960s when he was writing, he understood well that the routes he had surveyed, mapped out and engineered for Charles M. Upham in rural Thailand had become the routes into and out of the world's most violent confrontation with communism. He also knew that he'd served as Project Engineer Manager based in Bangkok, and that he'd been elevated to company vice-president at Upham headquarters back in Washington.

Looking at my father's typically unemotional listings of what all he accomplished in Thailand, it's unavoidable that we strain to see connections to the Vietnam War, whether they were really there or not. I suspect they were. History now tells us that U.S. involvement in Vietnam and the rest of Southeast Asia, whose exotic place names would become painfully familiar to Americans in the years ahead, began with advisers and covert operatives almost as soon as the French departed. Considerable groundwork for the war was laid during the Eisenhower administration, then was expanded mightily by JFK. That might explain a new concept that turns up in one of my father's descriptions of his work, with italics that I've added only now: "Advise and assist in planning a highway system in Thailand compatible with the present economic and security needs of the country."

So much of his resume language is familiar by now—planning, location, design, construction, maintenance, equipment, soils and materials—but this project on the eve of fully joined battle is the only reference I've found in my father's resume to "security."

There are two types of bound volumes I keep about my parents' four years in Thailand—a bright red leather-bound scrapbook my mother assembled of invitations to parties and other social functions, for there seemed to be someplace to go every night of the week among the movers and shakers, and the two-volume report my father put together for Upham and Upham presented to the government. On any given day, one or the other might make the more interesting reading.

The social book caught my eye early on, not least because it mirrored the busy life I saw my parents leading when I visited for the summer of 1961. That summer, as I was preparing for vacation from my studies at the University of Texas in Austin, nobody said, "That's next to *Vietnam*, isn't it? Isn't that place dangerous?" Ah, the summer of 1961 retained its innocence.

And certainly, danger seems far away in time and place when I look at these faded, brittle pages. Many of the invitations are written in Thai, a language so exoticly beautiful to look at on paper that I tried to take classes in it at Chulalongkorn, a place whose name made me smile because it rhymed with Longhorn. The president of the university, whose daughter worked as my father's secretary, talked Daddy out of encouraging me, saying, "Oh my, to learn Thai you have to be born a Thai."

There were many receptions for many dignitaries, and since my father headed up the respected highway delegation, my parents were apparently expected at all of them. They even met the King and Queen of Thailand on several occasions, though the main thing my father remembered was the King referring to his own children as "Thai-phoons."

Sometimes the dignitary came not from Thailand but from a great deal closer to our home. Lyndon B. Johnson, then serving as Kennedy's vice-president—the same job that had sent Nixon to Honduras—was scheduled to tour the American Embassy in Bangkok, so my father began pushing the idea of having LBJ speak to the local Rotary Club's Monday luncheon while he was in town. This the vice-president agreed to do, through several layers of handlers. In preparation, my father went to Johnson's hotel, the Erawan, in hopes of greeting his fellow Texan—which he got to do as the elevator doors swept open.

"Hello Lyndon," Daddy said. "You don't know me but I know you. You remember the ribbon-cutting at Buchanan Dam? And later at the barbecue they filled your plate as you reached over for your drink. The plate tipped and spilled gravy on your tie."

"Well," drawled LBJ, "you were there!"

↠ *Upham and Elmer in Thailand*

Both men had a good laugh about the memory, shared several thousand miles from Buchanan Dam deep in the Texas Hill Country.

Thrilled as Daddy was to see LBJ, another Texan's visit may have pleased him even more. As soon as he learned that his old Highway Department boss, D.C. Greer, was scheduled to give a talk in Australia, my father invited him to "stop by" on his way home. Only five years earlier, Greer had put in writing one of the kindest tributes to my father on the occasion of his first retirement.

After praising my father for his "more than thirty years of outstanding service" and in his continuing interest in the work of the Department, the legendary state highwayman wrote: "I want you to continue to feel that you will ever remain a part of this organization and that you will visit with us at any time you can."

Instead, it was Greer doing the visiting—on the other side of the world. My father put together a stylish reception for Greer with his counterparts in the Thai highway department, at the same Erawan hotel where he'd ambushed the vice-president in that elevator. "Needless to say," my father wrote later, "it was a huge success."

And of course, with my parents' nature, four years in Thailand provided plenty of weekends for their adventures. Sometimes traveling by car or flying when the distances were large, they toured the sights of exotic Penang, Singapore, Saigon, Laos, Chaing Mai, Phnom Penh, Hong Kong, Rangoon in Burma and the Gulf of Siam. One stop my father couldn't resist as a builder of roads and bridges was the broken remains of a World War II railway trestle crossing the river that separates Thailand from Burma. People who've read the book or seen the movie starring Alec Guinness know this span as *The Bridge Over the River Kwai.*

Their traveler's curiosity reaching full throttle, they even took a train with small sleeping cars to a forest north of Bangkok, near the border with Laos, for what my father invariably described as an "elephant hunt"—even though no elephant or any other creature was actually hunted. My parents and some friends got to watch what a Texan might call an elephant rodeo. The elephants seemed to be having a pretty good time.

Like every other report my father compiled for Upham, or later for TAMS or IESC, the two volumes about Thailand's almost non-existent highway system (presented to the Royal Thai Highway Department's colorfully named director, "Major General Sathien Pojananond") make for pretty dry reading.

Graphs fill page after page, and columns of measurements, and pen-and-ink drawings of things with names like "Road Drag Detail." The fact that at least some of these rehabilitated or new highways would soon deliver U.S. troops to Vietnam and even, in secret, to Laos, applies the silent witness of history to an engineer's head-down obsession with observable fact.

All of my father's work in Southeast Asia took place against the backdrop of a treaty pulled together immediately after the French defeat. Patterned in name and more after the NATO defense partnership in Western Europe, the 1954 agreement known as Southeast Asia Treaty Organization (SEATO) actually included only two Southeast Asian nations—Thailand and the Philippines.

The United States and all the other countries involved (France,

→ *Social life in Thailand*

Great Britain, New Zealand, Australia and Pakistan) were located someplace else, but clearly felt a Cold War stake in the region. As many had come to see it by then, at stake was the "containment" of communism. Theoretically, Vietnam, Cambodia and Laos might have joined the treaty, but they were forbidden by agreements reached in Geneva that same year.

As SEATO was headquartered in Bangkok, my father had many opportunities to work with and within its leadership. The alliance, it turns out, had few formal functions and, unlike NATO, no actual troops to send forth in the case of threat. That meant that, beyond any symbolic value SEATO might have in the fight against communism, its real value focused on raising economic foundations and living standards in Thailand and the rest of Southeast Asia. As before, leaders believed people who could feed their families and gaze at a roof over their heads were far less susceptible to communism than those who couldn't. Nothing did as much to deliver those conditions to Thailand as the roads, bridges and highways my father built there.

In retrospect, the alliance known as SEATO may have indeed raised the standards of living in all corners of the region. It connected Southeast Asia to the West and vice versa via student, scholar and cultural exchanges, and sponsored meetings and exhibitions throughout my father's assignment on all sorts of historical, cultural and religious topics.

At the same time, however, SEATO's provisions convinced the United States not to hold free elections in Vietnam in 1956, thus maintaining the division of North and South Vietnam at the 17th parallel. And their inclusion of Vietnam as a territory under SEATO protection gave the United States a legal and political cover for expanding involvement there in the early 1960s.

"The Vietnam War era was without question the most significant period in the history of relations between the United States and Thailand," writes historian Arne Kislenko. "After World War II the two countries developed an extremely close relationship premised on containing the spread of communism in Southeast Asia. For Thailand, the U.S. represented protection from the external threat of communist neighbors and the risk that an indigenous communist insurgency posed. For the U.S., Thailand represented a bastion of anti-communism in a region full of political uncertainty. It also represented a valuable Asian ally in the Cold War, a major 'rest and relaxation' (R&R) destination for U.S. servicemen in the region, a model of economic development in the so-called 'Third World,' and a strategic base from which to prosecute both overt and clandestine operations in Indochina...In this context, Thailand played an integral role in the shadows of the Vietnam War."

INTO THE
Jungle

CHAPTER ELEVEN

In 1962, at the height of John F. Kennedy's short-lived New Frontier, my father retired from Charles M. Upham as a company vice-president—only to sign on with a new company that would send him to many of the same kinds of countries, for all of the same kinds of reasons. For the final dozen years of Elmer Calvin's working life, he and my mother lived in Bolivia, Colombia, Turkey and Kuwait, all perceived in their day as battlegrounds in the war between democracy and communism. While Mother taught in American schools in each place, Daddy built roads and bridges in the face of old enemies and a few new ones, though I doubt anybody realized it at the time.

→ *Roads and relaxation in Bolivia*

Tippetts-Abbett-McCarthy-Stratton, happily referred to as TAMS, left behind a legacy of high-profile design and construction projects across the United States and abroad. For its part, after its charismatic founder's death, Upham's firm would be absorbed into the planning and consulting spinoff of Canadian Pacific Railways, only to be spun off as its own company in India by the 21st century, losing the last reference to "Upham" in its name.

→ *Bolivia's treacherous 'Highway of Death'*

One of TAMS' most visible projects was the "flying saucer" terminal so notable at the New York airport that came to be named for JFK, a "modern" design that earned 1960s icon status by welcoming the Beatles to America. Other work in planning and infrastructure stretched from traffic and parking in Boston's Back Bay to Burma and Nigeria. Years after my father's death, TAMS was even a claimant in a case against the Islamic Republic of Iran, which had come into violent existence only after my father's efforts at modernization there.

Typically, as with Upham, the "end users" of my father's work were the governments of the countries involved. Increasingly, though, as the world situation grew more complex, there were intermediaries as well, organizations with names like the Alliance for Progress, USAid and the World Bank. Generally, getting the contract for TAMS from such entities was somebody else's job; doing the work on the ground in the country was my father's. In that, his impressive resume preceded him.

The year before my parents left Dallas for Bolivia, the President announced the launch of the Alliance for Progress, which sought to improve the lives of Latin America's people. Nine days after that, he sent a message to Congress that led to the creation of the United States Government's Agency for International Development, known as USAid. Throughout the 1960s, that agency's program for Bolivia emphasized economic progress through the construction of road and airport infrastructure, not to mention the provision of basic human services. It also supported specific sectors such as mining, transport, agriculture and industry.

Perhaps we've forgotten now, but you couldn't get much closer to the Cold War's front lines than Bolivia in 1962—as my father understood from his work in Honduras, and as the President of the United States understood even better. The shadow of Castro's

Cuba was everywhere my father turned during his time in Bolivia from November 1962 to April 1965. The fear was that if the United States failed to support the latest "strong man" occupying the Presidential Palace, ragtag alliances of the poor, union workers and outside agitators who filled the jungles would stage a communist revolt of their own—and one more domino might topple, perhaps taking others with it. Indeed, within five years, the era's most legendary communist rebel would die in the same jungles my father tried to build highways through. Ernesto Che Guevara would be executed by the Bolivian military on the day of his capture in 1967, many believe with help from our CIA.

During those two-and-a-half years based in Cochabamba, my father was the chief engineer for a project financed by USAid. He worked with as many as fourteen U.S. engineers plus about three and hundred fifty Bolivian engineers and other workers. The result was a series of feasibility studies for about 2100 kilometers of new highways to be administered and maintained by the Ministry of Public Works. My father also, near the end of the contract, personally supervised the planning and construction of 145 new kilometers of roadway.

My father's time working in Bolivia, though it included several pleasant forays to peaceful villages high in the Andes, was among

→ *Meeting in South America*

the more frustrating periods of his career—primarily because, as our State Department said with admirable understatement, "The State of Bolivia has been a remarkably unsuccessful state." The country was poor and backward, ripe for social uprising. Which was sad, considering what my father came to know of its once-impressive history.

In pre-Colombian times, the area's high plains, known as the *Altiplano*, had an economy based upon irrigated agriculture; it was densely populated compared to other parts of South America. Not long after the Spanish conquest, silver deposits were discovered at Potosí and these silver mines made the region one of the wealthiest and most heavily populated in the entire empire. In 1800, Bolivia had a population that was second only to Brazil among the regions of South America. This wealth, however, never quite trickled down to the native population, who were forced to supply labor in the mines until the silver ran out and poverty returned. By the late 19th century, a new mining bonanza developed around tin, just about the time the world was discovering the convenience of canned food. This brought prosperity back to the old mining areas, and many great fortunes too.

By the time of my father's arrival, the troubled government was adopting themes that had been constant throughout his career. While tin remained a significant part of the Bolivian economy, both it and agriculture struggled to get their products to market—a situation that all agreed would be remedied by more and better roads. In addition, the government wanted to strengthen the identity of its people as one nation, rather than as members of this or that tribe living in the jungle, along a river or high in the mountains. Over the years, roads had demonstrated a special effectiveness in being the glue that held diverse populations together as a nationality.

Contrary to charges that revolutionaries like Guevara would make, the United States was anything but exploiting Bolivia.

Our country was actually subsidizing thirty percent of the government's central budget relative to its population, an amount of aid then greater than that sent to any other nation. Despite all the help from our country and the International Monetary Fund, the regime of Hernán Siles Zuazo was overwhelmed by opposition from the country's middle class, from tin miners and labor in general, and also from hostile farmers in remote areas. It was a horrible time trying to accomplish anything in Bolivia, but the Kennedy administration was committed.

From the standpoint of adventure, the most memorable portion of my father's Bolivian assignment occurred in the two weeks leading up to July 4, 1963: something his special report to TAMS referred to as "Ground Reconnaissance Project 28." My father spent virtually that entire time riding mules up and down mountains, forging streams and rivers and seeking alternate routes for roads that were already being discussed. This physically demanding trek into the bush was necessary, he recalled, because the last report on the Rio Tipuani Valley was compiled by a British geologist known only as "Mr. Evans," who was searching for minerals, rather than routes. He had covered this ground, probably with the same means of conveyance, back in 1902.

The group—my father and another TAMS engineer—packing tents and simple cooking equipment, left La Paz by Jeep on June 25. They were accompanied by a guide named Marcelo Peinado, later proclaimed invaluable in dealing with tribes they encountered along the way. For his part, Peinado had been briefed on the region by "Father Zachary," a Franciscan friar. In making their way to Sorata and Tipuani, and then on to Zongo in the Rio Zongo Valley, the party traveled up to 15,000 feet above sea level, where my father recorded, "the foundation changed to broken boulders of gray granite interspersed with strata of firm shale." Within a day or so, they had to leave the Jeeps behind and rendezvous with their mules.

→ *Busy Latin bus terminal*

Day after grueling day of riding and hiking passed in the Bolivian high country, each one marked by blisters a little different from the previous day's. My father, formed a "city boy," noted that he and his fellow engineer were not up to trails built originally by Incas and little improved by their Spanish conquerors. As their notes for future road construction filled page after page, they realized just how different this mission was from the one carried out four centuries earlier.

"This trail was constructed soon after the Spaniards arrived in 1532, and they were no doubt searching for minerals," Daddy wrote, thinking of the dreams of gold that gathered under the magical Spanish words "*El Dorado.*" "They must have exploited the Indians and had them seesaw up and down the slopes by cutting through each stratum or formation and thus do prospecting as the trail was built." Referring to his own sixty-two-year-old body's aches and pains, my father had to add with a suppressed wink: "There can be little wonder as to why the Incas are extinct after constructing and walking such trails."

I'm not sure how much my father managed to accomplish during his time in Bolivia, primarily because everything our country was doing there seemed to depend on the Zuazo government remaining in power—which it didn't, being overthrown by the military in 1964. By then, however, my parents had moved on to Colombia, hoping for greater impact and more measurable success.

In retrospect, the approximately $100 million poured into Bolivia for road construction only served to underline the extreme deficiencies on the receiving end. As two American historians wrote later:

> "The poor performance of the entire agricultural sector, however, belies the elaborate and expensive cost-benefit studies which attempt to economically justify road projects. Roads are favored over other projects because of the attempt to integrate the culturally diverse and geographically dispersed segments of Bolivian society and thus serve the national corporate state. However, there exists abundant evidence of the unplanned, inefficient and unproductive nature of Bolivia's transportation development."

Certainly, those were things my father and his fellow TAMS engineers worked even harder to avoid once settled into Colombia, making their way into the hinterland from their headquarters in Bogotá. The fact that my parents spent close to four years in the country speaks to a more committed long-term relationship with the United States. But

→ *Colombian Cathedral*

then again, their time coincided with two unexpected developments there: the beginnings of the guerilla movement, the Revolutionary Armed Forces of Colombia, that would teach the world the dreaded acronym FARC, as well as the evolution and eventual demise of the Alliance for Progress.

According to its TAMS contract, financed by the World Bank, my father worked with Colombia's Ministry of Public Works, and the larger government, to plan a complete reorganization of the maintenance division since keeping the roads passable through difficult terrain was a daunting problem, as well as to study the feasibility of various new roads and large bridges. As usual in my father's career, such planning put him at the center of everything that followed: route studies, construction plans and specifications, evaluation of bids and supervision of the actual construction.

The most memorable non-work activity in Colombia was the trip my father and mother took to the southernmost tip of the country, where solid ground quickly gave way to the Amazon River surrounded by views of Colombia as well as Peru and Bolivia. There, in a village called Leticia, my parents met up with an American from Florida who was collecting animal specimens for a university in the Midwest. The American, remembered only as "Mike" in my father's notes, served as mayor, banker and postmaster of Leticia, and he served as guide on an adventure that included a toast upon crossing the equator, a special dinner and a nighttime alligator hunt on the Amazon.

My father never forgot that hunt in a small boat driven by an outboard motor, the steering handled by a small Colombian boy taking direction from Mike. And he never forgot the sight of those "coals of fire," the eyes of alligators watching from the deep-black Amazonian darkness. The hunters picked up eight to ten alligators—presumably on the small side—and my father requested two. "Upon our return to Bogotá," he wrote in his notes, "I had an Italian shoemaker make a pair of alligator shoes for Agnes."

About the time of my parents' arrival, Colombia began to figure in extensive diplomatic correspondence focused on two distinct but related areas. Efforts such as those by TAMS, USAid and the Alliance set about winning "hearts and minds" by way of roads and infrastructure, in addition to education, medical care and other services. At least equally important, were the military and paramilitary efforts of U.S. soldiers to help the Colombian government eradicate small, poorly armed rebel groups gathered in remote villages of the southern Andes. As in Honduras, the enemy wasn't merely those rebels, but the specter of Soviet-style communism.

"Communists [in] these areas are genuine and not crypto-communists," wrote one Bogotá-based U.S. diplomat, referencing a letter from Colombia's president. These insurgents, he insisted, were "oriented toward Cuba whence they receive direction and financing."

At one point, U.S. General William Yarborough, founder of the Green Berets, toured Colombia with some of his fighters and, in a "secret supplement" to his official report, suggested that Special Forces detachments be assigned to the Colombian military. These, he wrote, should train Colombian paramilitary hunter-killer squads called *localizadores* to "perform counter-agent and counter-propaganda functions and as necessary execute paramilitary, sabotage, and/or terrorist activities against known communist proponents."

→ *Elmer and Agnes meet the TAMS clients*

By seeing the communist threat as organized and monolithic, the U.S. and its allies failed to distinguish among the Moscow-oriented FARC and what would soon become the Castro-leaning National Liberation Army (ELN) and the Chinese-Maoist People's Liberation Army (EPL). Whenever Colombia's military occupied villages and towns controlled by one of these groups, they did so only temporarily. The moment they left, the villages returned to rebel control.

If anything, such U.S.-advised military operations are now seen as forcing small, sedentary gangs of discontents to become a mobile guerilla army. The violence that followed, linking up later with Colombia's active drug cartel based around Medellín, would not lessen until the beginning of the 21st century.

Perhaps worst of all, historians now believe the $732 million dispersed in Colombia by the Alliance for Progress while my father was there had the effect of protecting the government from seeing the error of its ways. Not only were human rights largely ignored in Colombia, but so was the wild discrepancy in living conditions brought about by wealth amid so much abject poverty. To its credit, the United States repeatedly drew up plans for agrarian land reform and presented them to the Colombian government. But after a certain point in the mid-1960s, with the Alliance itself under scrutiny, the Colombians did little but collect the U.S.'s dollars.

There was nothing not to like about the Alliance for Progress, in theory. President Kennedy was reasonable to hope, after his considerable study of Latin America and its diverse peoples, that anti-poverty aid would increase the legitimacy of national governments while preventing a series of communist revolutions—in other words, preventing more Cubas. The fact that the Alliance failed to deliver its promised material improvement, democracy and stability is generally blamed on a number of interesting factors.

The most eye-catching is, of course, the assassination of

Kennedy and the rise to the presidency of Texan Lyndon B. Johnson. Johnson was a different kind of leader and a different kind of man, even more pragmatic and certainly less idealistic about his country's role on the world stage. Gazing at the Alliance as he inherited it, LBJ found a lack of political will on the part of our Latin American partners, a broad unwillingness to make the social and economic reforms the United States hoped its money would subsidize. He also found bureaucracies in both Washington and Latin America that had trouble accomplishing what they said they would, against the backdrop of a problem far larger than they ever said it would be.

After all, Europe had been rebuilt under the Marshall Plan— why not Latin America? Building it proved much harder than rebuilding. All these issues might have brought down the Alliance for Progress by the time my parents wrapped up their years in Colombia, but by that point, the United States was focusing virtually all its money, energy and political will on: Vietnam.

The Alliance for Process was done by the time my father turned his eyes from Latin America at the end of the 1960s, though other Kennedy-era initiatives like the Partners for the Americas and the Peace Corps would enjoy longer lives. In some cases, volunteers for those two groups did good work by traversing roads and bridges my father designed, contracted and constructed. His final two assignments as a highway engineer, however, would take him far from the jungles of the New World to what were becoming new battlefields at the very crossroads of the Old.

ANCIENT
Crossroads

CHAPTER TWELVE

For more thousands of years than most of us can count, the area we know as Turkey, called Asia Minor by scholars, was a land bridge between East and West. And for most of those millennia, conquerors crossed from either direction with huge armies: Alexander and his Greeks followed later by Caesar and his Romans from the West, Cyrus and Darius of the Persian Empire from the

→ *Atatürk Mausoleum in Ankara*

East. Eventually the region developed empires of its own.

First the Byzantines, and finally the Ottomans, were based there. And for centuries, the dazzling city known as Byzantium, later as Constantinople, was the center of the known universe. During World War I, the tired, crumbling Ottomans chose their friends poorly and lost much when the German Kaiser surrendered. Yet something good came out of the debacle.

A young army officer named Mustafa Kemal Atatürk led a revolution in the early 1920s, set up a new style of democratic republic and sought to align his Turkey not with the repressive East but with the progressive West, Europe and the United States. My father headed to Turkey in February 1969, with my mother following, as usual, a few weeks later.

There was snow on the ground in the capital in Ankara, as

there probably wouldn't have been in the Mediterranean former capital of Istanbul—the name the late Kemal (by now known as Atatürk, "Father of Turks") gave to Byzantium/Constantinople. It was symbolism he felt was important, building a new capital in the stark but pure Anatolian heartland, rather than accepting the corrupt international machinations of his country's past. As usual with a TAMS contract, my father was there to "assist and advise" the Turkish government on its roads and bridges, and to help them set up a streamlined, modern department to build and maintain them. After his experience in Texas all those years ago, this should not have been challenging. But Turkey was a long way from Texas.

My father's notes, gathered during my parents' two years based in Ankara and traveling to the hinterland, also show a keen interest in the importance this land played throughout history. On weekend excursions, my parents paid visits to the alleged Tomb of King Midas (later deciding it probably wasn't) and the town of Gordium, where Alexander the Great faced a thick knotted rope he'd been challenged to untie and then chopped it in half with his sword—antiquity's Gordian Knot. My father had my mother snap his photo tying his own Gordian Knot.

"I still have it," he wrote of that photo years later, "unless someone has carelessly thrown in away with all my National Geographic maps, which I had collected since 1926." By this point in his life, however, he had spent time in many parts of the world most Americans knew only from *National Geographic.*

He and my mother enjoyed the weird rock smokestacks of inland Göreme, where some of Asia Minor's earliest Christians carved out places to live and pray. They made trips outside Turkey to see Thessalonica in the Macedonian section of Greece (area where the apostle Paul directed his letters known to Bible readers as 1st and 2nd Thessalonians). They also visited Beirut and Cyprus—areas which reminded them of the conflict that always seems to wait for humanity over history's next hill.

On July 20, 1969, my father pressed his ear against a German radio he'd purchased in Ankara, listening to the *Voice of America* announcer take him moment by moment through Neil Armstrong's first steps onto the moon. As an American and an engineer, he was proud of NASA's magnificent achievement. "No," he recorded in his notes, "I wasn't there in person. But in spirit, yes."

Though Turkey had spent most of World War II as a neutral country before declaring war on Germany at the end, it emerged during the Cold War as a strategic testing ground for U.S. vs. Soviet power and will. Geography alone would mandate no less, thus returning Turkey to its role as land bridge and this time a connection between a divided Europe and the oil-rich and volatile Middle East. Turkey had a tradition of highways begun under Atatürk, who rightly believed they would encourage state building and commerce at the same time. My father discovered these highways, bridges and rural roads were uneven in terms of quality, many having been allowed to crumble toward impassability except by the donkey carts that still made up the "auto inventory" of many remote areas.

Working with other TAMS consultants, my father blamed inconsistent building materials and inferior methods, and then he drew up a plan for organizing and improving. The goal was an entirely revamped "federal" highway system—much like the one he'd traveled all over North Texas planning in the Age of the American Interstate.

Building what amounted to an interstate through some of the earth's most ancient lands had its spiritual and emotional rewards. Much of his work centered on creating, connecting and upgrading what came to be known as the Trans Turkey Highway: 3,200 kilometers beginning at the border of Soviet-

↳ *Highway bridge in Turkey*

→ *Fishing boats along the Turkish coast*

controlled Bulgaria and passing across the Bosphorus waterway at Istanbul (the boundary between Europe and Asia) to head east to Ankara. At a point just beyond there, the highway split: one branch led to the Syrian border, another to the Iraqi border, and yet another branch would head off all the way to Turkey's border with Iran.

In Syria, Iraq and Iran—even in 1969, there was absolutely no doubt among my father and his coworkers about the importance of these places to the future of the world. While the English of a later Turkish description isn't perfect, the scope of my father's mission in those two years is clear. "The improvement program aforementioned doesn't require the construction of new roads," the report states. "The main purpose of the program is to enhance the physical standards of the road in order to make it sufficient for the traffic. During the works slight geometric improvements...some safety measures are taken into consideration." All the Republic of Turkey was looking for, it turns out, was *Good Roads*.

My father's contract came to an end in Turkey in February, 1971. Since TAMS had an official retirement age of sixty-five, and he was only months from turning seventy, he decided to finally take retirement. While this was taking place, however, a group called the International Executive Service Corps was tracking him down. To this day, IESC does a good job of supplying companies around the world with executives, most often retired high-quality personnel looking for a challenge. Part of me can't imagine why my father went, after all he'd accomplished in so many corners of the globe. Yet even in their seventies, he and my mother were always ready for an adventure—like the one that awaited them in Kuwait on the crucial Persian Gulf.

After a long flight from Dallas, within minutes of their arrival my parents were being driven by an assigned guide through scenes that looked both exotic and familiar. After Texas, of course, the

→ *Iconic scenes from Kuwait*

whole idea of a desert that ended at the edge of blue water was rare, yet few things could have seemed as familiar to these Texans as this landscape spotted with oil wells. Their guide, a Palestinian hired to work in Kuwait, told them that oil was the only real business in Kuwait—not to mention the primary source of wealth for its hereditary leader, called the Emir.

The client on the IESC contract, Kharafi Industries, was a large construction company based in Kuwait but with various activities purportedly stretching into Saudi Arabia, Abu Dhabi, Bahrain, Dubai and Muscat. The family owning the firm had made its initial fortune in pearl diving—Kuwait's most important pre-oil business—but it now dealt in housing construction, road building and even metal furniture. What Kharafi wanted was clear enough: "Civil engineer experienced in construction management to recommend ways and means to streamline present system of management and/or reorganize it."

My father started streamlining in a hurry. Procuring a Saudi visa for him proved impossible, which took that country off his assignment sheet. Other places fell off when Daddy found no appreciable Kharafi work going on there. That left only the Kharafis' homebase.

"Kuwait will be hot when you get there," IESC director Ralph C. Shaffer had written to my father three months earlier, "but all the buildings are air-conditioned. The Hilton is most pleasant with all kinds of recreation—swimming, bowling, tennis, etc. Kuwait is interesting these days. It has good English bookshops, a museum, cinemas, etc."

In 1971, when my father arrived in Kuwait for his career's final assignment, those English shopkeepers were in the process of pulling out—and the symbolism couldn't have been more explicit. Since the beginning of the 20th century, Great Britain had been the western power to reckon with in the Middle East, a region still noteworthy for historical documents like the Balfour Declaration and for landmarks like the Allenby Bridge. Many, if not most, of the efforts to achieve peace and stability in the region had been conducted over the decades with a British accent. Still, the end of World War II had marked the rise of American power, and even fifteen years after the Suez Crisis, Britain retained neither the will nor the creativity to seek peace where there didn't ever seem to be any.

English fingerprints remained everywhere in Kuwait, including the country's very existence and placement on the map. Beginning in ancient times and as late as 1899, Kuwait was a center of trade on a tiny corner of the Persian Gulf—a body of water that connected buyers and sellers in India, Africa, Mesopotamia and the Levant. In that year, with a nod from its Sabah ruling dynasty, Kuwait signed a treaty with the United Kingdom giving the British considerable say over policy in return for protection and an annual subsidy, all prompted by concerns that a planned Berlin-Baghdad Railway would give the Germans control over the Gulf. Soon after the start of World War I, Britain declared Kuwait an independent principality under its protection.

Oil was discovered in Kuwait in 1938, only five years after its discovery in Saudi Arabia, two years before Qatar, twenty-four before Abu Dhabi and twenty-nine before Dubai, propelling what had been dusty villages and rundown trading ports to the forefront of wealth and privilege. These discoveries would also affect my father's work in Kuwait in the form of the Organization of Petroleum Exporting Countries. OPEC was formed in 1960 by Iran, Iraq, Kuwait, Saudi Arabia and Venezuela, but only lately had begun flexing its muscles over U.S. support for Israel. Kuwait became independent of Great Britain in 1961, quickly becoming the largest exporter of oil in the Persian Gulf.

With my father's arrival, the United States was making several statements at once. By this point, the Eisenhower Doctrine had become the Nixon Doctrine. This current version, while still communist-centric, emphasized supporting strong allies in areas that would prove strategic, rather than sending in U.S. troops in the combat-averse post-Vietnam era. Roads and bridges would be ideal, it was felt by Washington's now-aging Cold Warriors, for cementing Kuwait's fidelity to the West against any advances the Soviets might consider.

Such improvements would also help Kuwait defend itself against one or all of its much larger, much more aggressive neighbors: Iraq, Iran and Saudi Arabia. Iraq in particular treated Kuwait as one of its provinces—the only one with access to the sea, as Britain had intentionally drawn the map back in 1913. Iraq made moves against Kuwait as early as its independence, but in 1961 the British military stood in its way. By 1990, as we now know, Iraq's dictator would occupy Kuwait until the allies of Desert Storm drove him out.

"All of us remember just four years ago," my father wrote after Desert Storm, remembering his three months traveling the same terrain, "when Saddam Hussein invaded defenseless Kuwait and torched their oil wells. That was highway robbery by your next door neighbor." Then, as a proud Texan, he just couldn't resist: "Soon after the Gulf War, I read that Kuwait employed Red Adair from Houston/Beaumont to finally put out the fires."

→ *Across the Golden Horn in Istanbul*

THE ROAD
Home

CHAPTER THIRTEEN

All I knew about my parents in their retirement was that I loved them, that I missed them as a daily part of my existence, that their letters and cards full of advice to me and their grandsons meant everything, and that each time I went to visit them on Beverly Drive they seemed to have new and exciting stories to share. I chose to focus on those stories from home, from church, from various society functions, rather than on the fact that my parents seemed smaller each time I saw them. This was especially true of Daddy, the tall, slender young highway engineer my mother fell in love with.

↳ *Enjoying retirement in Dallas*

They kept up a keen interest in foreign affairs—especially as events impacted the dozen or so countries they'd come to know quite well. Considering the strategic Cold War underpinning of their travels, those countries frequently appeared in the news as hot spots.

My parents were deeply saddened by the Watergate scandal that forced the resignation of President Richard Nixon—not least because of Nixon's efforts while in the White House to end the Cold War he'd once done so much to inflame. It was remarkable, for a man who'd imagined communists hiding everywhere, including the State Department, to achieve what he called "peace with honor" in Vietnam, to open talks with "Red China" and to successfully negotiate nuclear arms with the Soviet Union. "I hope and pray," my father told anyone who would listen, "there will never be another nuclear bomb exploded in a conflict between nations." With so many beloved faces from the Manhattan Project now passing into eternity, my father understood his hope and prayer better than most. When all else seemed to fail, he relied on a single line from Ephesians 4:32, "Be ye kind, one to another."

My parents were also hopeful that the significant strides toward peace in the Middle East that Nixon made would eventually take hold. Presidents Carter and Clinton would make strides too, though the voices of these "better angels" were drowned out by other, hate-filled choruses.

My father's curiosity about new technology got the better of him at one point, and it had nothing to do with book clubs or bridge parties. It had to do with computers, a type of machinery he had shaped his entire half-century career without. While he was still young enough to drive the distance by himself, he

headed to College Station for an introductory computer class with fellow senior citizens. An article published at A&M, with a photo of my father gazing at a screen as a young female instructor looked on, described Elmer Calvin as the oldest person to take the class. *Class of 1924*, he would have reminded her.

In July of 1987, my father decided that College Station wasn't far enough—he wanted to make one more trip abroad, to the country he'd been taught to hate and fear more

→ *Elmer's computer class at A&M*   than any other. Even though he'd lived and worked in no fewer than three countries adjacent to the Soviet Union, his Cold War sense of justice had prevented him from considering a visit. In the mid-1980s, as the Soviets faced their own internal problems and began a gradual "thaw" in their relations with the free world, my father decided he could wait no longer.

My mother had recently broken her hip, so even though she was recovering well at home, she opted out of the demanding trip. She and I gave my father our blessings, letting him sign onto a tour organized by the Texas Society of Professional Engineers. The group of forty was mostly from Texas and Arkansas, though my father's assigned roommate was much younger, about forty, a high school teacher from near Philadelphia. He was, my father recorded with some relief, "of high morals, a non-smoker and a non-drinker."

As best I can tell from Daddy's notes, the trip was the Soviet "grand tour, 1980s-style," beginning with a flight from JFK to Helsinki and then on to Moscow. During several days of sightseeing—Red Square, St. Basil's Cathedral with its rainbow of onion domes, the Kremlin, Lenin's Tomb—the group was based at the mammoth, in elegant Hotel Russia, which my father couldn't miss noting "accommodates 6,000 people."

Other parts of the itinerary included Vladamir, Suzdal ("TV," my father wrote, "was about what we had in the late 1940s or early 1950s"), then bussing back to Moscow for a flight to Yalta in the Crimea on the Black Sea. The Crimean War (whose famous battle had inspired the poem "The Charge of the Light Brigade"), would have been familiar to Daddy, as well as a later significance that hit much closer to home. Yalta was the site of a crucial World War II meeting between FDR, Churchill and Stalin, in which they essentially divvied up the postwar world. If the Cold War my father had fought so diligently had a birthplace, it was Yalta.

The tour's final leg took my father and friends north again to

Leningrad, known at various times as St. Petersburg. There was some major sightseeing in this city made opulent by the czars and czarinas of old Russia: the summer palaces of Peter the Great and Catherine the Great, the Hermitage, the Winter Palace. His notes on that final stop take the tone of the engineer: "It covers more than a large city block. Each large room is filled with framed paintings and sculptures of noted painters. One large room has solid malachite columns and a table about 7 feet by 4 feet, 2 inches, this of beautiful malachite."

I still treasure the postcards Daddy sent to Mother and me from the Soviet Union. One favorite he mailed to my mother from Leningrad: "My Dear Sweetheart. Darling, I so hope you are still improving. I love you dearly… All of us are homesick but I am having a wonderful time. With love from Russia and love from me —Elmer." On the card he sent to me from Yalta, he used the salutation I always favored, and even got the James Bond title right: "Dear Little Sweetheart. Hope all of you are OK. I so hope Mama is improving and wishing she could be with me on this trip… From Russia with Love, Daddy."

After his return to the United States via Helsinki, my father mused on all he had taken in. He felt that some of the Kremlin's willingness to cooperate with the West grew out of President Reagan's strong stands, as well as the probability that the nuclear disaster at Chernobyl had shown them "how devastating a nuclear war could be." Our country's knowledge of the Soviet Union's financial self-destruction came two years after my father's visit, when the once-impenetrable Iron Curtain came tumbling down.

Even as a Cold Warrior, my father tried hard to square what he'd believed for so many years with what he saw. "The U.S. news media continues to report the superiority of Russia's army, navy and air force equipment and armament, which is probably true. However, their technology must be weak, since it is reported they are always trying to steal our technology and secrets. And if their military technology is no better than that observed in the civilian category, we should have less worries and fear."

Having lived so much of his adult live in tense, silent conflict with the Soviets, my father hopefully found a measure of peace by taking his own advice.

With a less active social calendar than my mother kept, my father spent his free time in retirement doing the things he loved. These included polishing rocks and gemstones he'd found on various adventures around the globe—he loved to refer to himself as an "amateur lapidarian" —and I can still picture him hunched over this or that chunk of earth, working away. In 1984, he donated a large quartz crystal to the College of Geosciences at A&M, which promised to give the piece a suitable mounting and display it with a brass plaque in their collection. A photograph of the display was among my father's papers at the time of his death.

What Daddy did most in retirement was to instruct his grandsons about what it meant to be a man—which to him meant being honest, hard-working, ambitious and faithful to your God and your country. I still have a few of those notes and the clips of writings he attached to them, sometimes tongue-in-cheek, sometimes serious, always concerned about the two boys who would grow up in a world that didn't seem to teach them the lessons his world, beginning in Markley, had taught him.

The poem "Desiderata" figured in to his advice, encouraging the boys to be captains of their own ships, masters of their own souls. Several times he copied, and once even re-typed, a motivational piece called "The Art of Getting Along," explaining that either his mother or Aunt Wilda had clipped it from some magazine and given it to him when he was at Graham High. He explained as well why he kept writing: "I love you two boys very much, and I am counting on your futures."

Later, my father sent my sons a photo of the rugged and rusted carpenter's square his father had used in 1900 to build the family farm. Explaining in an official-looking "memo" that he still kept the square in his workshop in Dallas, my father used it as a launching pad for a lecture on pursuing life goals while sticking to the "straight and narrow," as well as being "straight" with others in all business and personal dealings. "And oh yes," he finishes the memo, "don't forget to call your mother!"

My mother recovered from her first hip fracture, but now in her mid-90s, a second proved more than she could bear. As I remember it, she was walking through a social event when she tripped on a rug and tumbled. Agnes Standlee Calvin died at age 96 at the Baylor Institute for Rehabilitation on August 7, 1994. In its news story on my mother's passing, the *Dallas Morning News* quoted me on the meaning of her globetrotting life. "She was exposed to multi-culturalism back then by seeing cultures that others were not able to see. She was also able to teach what she learned throughout her full life."

That, certainly, was one kind of epitaph. Another turned up among my father's papers, a card he'd given my mother on one of her birthdays along with ruby earrings ("to match your sparkling eyes") and a ruby pendant ("to match your pure heart"). Daddy must have gone back to this card after she was gone, to the typed note he titled "To the Best and Sweetest Wife in the Whole World" and signed at the bottom, "From your loving husband, Calvin." Most of all, I'm sure he thought often about the memory he used to begin his birthday greeting. "After my mother met you," he wrote to Agnes, "she said to me 'You could not have found a better or nicer girl in the world.'" The woman that all relations called "Aunt Lillie" proved to be right about Agnes, as she was about so many things over the years.

My father needed my help more and more around the house, and also for getting to the places in Dallas he was convinced he needed to go. This was especially true after he tried to back out of our driveway but stepped on the gas instead of the brake,

→ *Agnes shares her stories of travel*

lurching across the street into a neighbor's tree. I thanked God neither my father nor anyone else was injured that day. Sensibly, Daddy gave up his car keys and driver's license after that.

Frequently, we found ourselves talking about years past, about jobs he'd handled for the Texas Highway Department and the Corps of Engineers; about what he always called our "exodus" from Egypt; and about the many places he and my mother had lived for Upham, for TAMS, for IESC. I decided it was finally time to write these things down, so I encouraged him to tell me about the little moments he thought were memorable, the people they met, the good works they accomplished over so many years. I typed up what he told me, and gave them the titles he designated, such as "My Assignment in Iran—Last Half of 1958," or "Our Pleasant

Four Years in Thailand." In those moments, listening to my father open up to his only child about his truly remarkable life, I decided I needed to share his story more widely.

In the end, as a kind of blessing, my father never spent much time in any hospital. He'd been admitted with pneumonia adding to his asthma—I think he was treated no more than a day, though I could be wrong—and had emerged seeming more fit than ever, though none of us who loved him could imagine how that might be. But then, when the pneumonia returned and filled his lungs, Daddy was the first to decide it was his time. He went into the hospital then, instructed me to call all the cousins and his grandsons, and made me promise I'd do nothing out of the ordinary to keep him alive. My father knew, I suspect, he'd never be returning to 4437 Beverly Drive.

Our family gathered, each receiving his or her goodbye at Daddy's bedside. I noticed that he didn't seem sad. He also didn't seem frightened, certainly not by anything that might lie ahead. He may have even seemed a little bit happy, light years removed from whatever had overcome him that day in Markley when he'd bent over to clutch those pieces of earth. And as he breathed his last on April 7, 1997, I thought that just maybe I understood his emotion that day.

At long last, Elmer and Agnes, husband and wife, my father and my mother, could travel together, embracing some new adventure, once again.

→ *World travelers at home*

→ *Agnes, Carolyn and Elmer*

A LEGACY

I've heard it said, and I believe it's true: Once our parents have left us, the elements that remain are their values. Those values may strike us as primitive at times, maybe simplistic; yet as we age we come to realize that so many of the best things we've accomplished, contributed and stood up for in life echo the values our parents struggled to impart. I am proud that my father tried to communicate his values to his grandsons during his final years. And I am proud of them for trying to adhere to those values.

→ *Elmer Ben Calvin*

What are these values? Do they still serve us, or should they perhaps be buried with the men and women who lived and died for them? At the risk of sounding like an engineer's daughter, here are six values I've identified as essential to my parents' time—indeed to the lives of most members of their generation.

The Value of Education. My mother was a school teacher for twenty-six years on four continents. In our family, the value of education was obvious and assumed. My father attributed every bit of his success to his mother, mostly for making sure he went to school. Whether it was Graham High or Texas A&M, or even the law classes he took later, my parents filled me with the faith that no learning is ever wasted. These days, there seems to be doubt about this—and nowhere more pathetically than among "self-made" men and women. We are never truly "self-made." There is a God who gives us life, and then there are people who guide us, correct us and inspire us. We call those people teachers.

The Value of Unity. Just as my mother connected students with their futures, my father understood that roads and bridges brought people together. In some ways, these bits of engineering accomplished society's ultimate connection: towns and rural areas to cities, people with products to people who needed them, and people who longed to feel part of something greater than what they could see. Elmer Calvin built roads and bridges, but he and others also built a new way of being Americans that had, in theory, been the idea all along: One nation. Roads and bridges help people view each other with less suspicion. Our country could certainly use some unity right now.

→ *Agnes Standlee Calvin*

The Value of Sacrifice. My parents started life together during the Great Depression. There was much good fortune in my father's career, certainly. Yet my parents, like most Americans during those terrible times, responded to setbacks with sacrifice, by simply doing without. Each generation, I believe, faces its own challenges; but the sacrifices our forebearers made during the Depression were the only forces profound enough to prepare them for World War II. In each of our times of doing without, we should be able to take solace in the fact that those before us not only survived deprivation but overcame it.

The Value of Honesty. Emerging from both the Depression and global conflict, Americans like my parents embraced peace with spectacular ambition. They built more, bigger and better and faster, and they bought more for less money to enjoy life with as well. Yet one truth they never forgot was the importance of personal honesty. The straight and narrow, they called it, sometimes pretending to complain. Others called it "playing by the rules." In my parents' America, you always played by the rules. I can only imagine how much better our world would be if my generation and those that came after us had chosen to do the same.

The Value of Strength. My parents lived through global warfare that killed fifty million people, that savaged families around the world. Death was as close on every battlefield in Europe or the Pacific as it was on every residential street, arriving in an official car and with a knock at your door. My parents believed America had to defend itself, both in the 1940s and in what President Kennedy later called "the long twilight struggle" of the Cold War. There was no hesitancy in my parents' belief, no uncertainty. Still, growing up, I never got the sense they glorified war. Having lived with the real thing, and having lost so much in the defense of freedom, my parents, I believe, took combat seriously. It was never a whim, never a posture, never a game. Their example should prevent it from becoming any of those things today.

The Value of America. My parents believed in this country, in the immensity of its idealism, in the scope of its potential greatness, in the importance of its mission. The truths upon which the United States was founded were my parents' truths, pure and simple. America was meant to be a light to the world, even beyond that torch held aloft to immigrants across the ages. Americans like my parents labored to build trade around the world, to create democratic partners and to build sustainable economies.

Coming of age in a time of global war, they spent the rest of their lives hoping to be instruments of peace. Committed to the vision of a world improved by each individual's effort, my father the engineer and my mother the teacher built highways to the world.

FAMILY
Timeline

1871 Robert John Calvin (Elmer's father) born in Markley, Texas.

1879 Lillie Cooley (Elmer's mother) born in Graham, Texas.

1898 Agnes Beatrice Standlee (Elmer's wife) born in Cornelius, Oregon.

1901 Elmer Ben Calvin born in Markley.

1910 John Robert Calvin (Elmer's brother) born in Markley.

1916 Elmer enters Graham High School.

1920 Elmer graduates from GHS and enters Texas A&M, joining Corps of Cadets.

1924 Elmer graduates from Texas A&M with B.S. in civil engineering. Goes to work for Texas Highway Department, in Shackelford and Throckmorton counties and then in Austin. Part of WPA-funded "golden age" of highway and bridge construction.

1926 Elmer and Agnes meet in Albany and marry. Also, Elmer becomes life member of American Society of Civil Engineers in New York.

1941 Elmer and Agnes have a daughter, Carolyn. Also, Agnes earns her Masters of Education degree from what is now Texas State University.

1942 Elmer begins active duty with U.S. Army Corps of Engineers, constructing expedited military facilities in Central Texas, including Camp Hood (now Fort Hood).

1943 Elmer cleared for Top Secret work and appointed as Design and Construction Engineer for General Groves on Manhattan Project in Oak Ridge, Tennessee.

1945 Elmer assigned by General Groves to Philadelphia to expedite orders for Manhattan Project. Successful test of nuclear bomb at Alamogordo, New Mexico. First and second atomic bombs dropped on Hiroshima and Nagasaki, bringing end of World War II.

1946 Elmer returns from military service to Texas Highway Department, enjoys second "golden age," including planning and construction of interstate highways.

1950 Elmer retires from Army as Lieutenant Colonel; was in army reserves at the time.

1951 Elmer and Carolyn move to 4437 Beverly Dr. in Dallas, their permanent home.

1956 Elmer retires from Texas Highway Department and joins Charles M. Upham Associates. First assignment with Agnes and Carolyn, to Cairo, Egypt. Family evacuated from Alexandria by U.S. Navy during Suez Crisis.

1957 Elmer assigned to Honduras, going with Upham to improve highway system and bridges as part of U.S. aid amid concern over Castro's growing revolution in Cuba.

1957 Earle and Mary retire to Dallas, though he continues to practice and teach medicine for many years.

1958 Elmer travels alone and in secret to Iran, consulting for Upham with Shah's government on infrastructure of remote and ancient Kerman Province.

1959 Elmer and Agnes begin four-year residence in Bangkok, Thailand, consulting on road construction, including in remote areas near Laos border, in what proved to be buildup to Vietnam War.

1960 Elmer elected vice-president of Charles M. Upham.

1963 Elmer retires from Charles M. Upham and joins Tippetts-Abbett-McCarthy-Stratton for first assignment in Bolivia. Elmer cleared by U.S. government for USAid work there.

1965 Also with TAMS, Elmer and Agnes relocate to Bogotá, Colombia.

1969 TAMS assigns Elmer and Agnes to Turkey for two years, based in the capital of Ankara, to consult on modernizing highway system for republic straddling Europe and Asia.

1974 After retirement from TAMS, Elmer and Agnes accept brief consulting assignment to Kuwait with International Executive Service Corps.

1975 Elmer and Agnes retire to Dallas.

1976 Elmer and Agnes celebrate 50 years of marriage.

1987 Elmer travels alone on Texas Society of Professional Engineers tour of Soviet Union.

1994 Agnes Standlee Calvin dies in Dallas at age 96.

1997 Elmer Ben Calvin dies in Dallas at age 95.

ACKNOWLEDGEMENTS

The authors would like to thank and credit the sources below for their help in the research and writing of this book:

PEOPLE

Thank you to Carolyn's cousins who contributed not only encouragement but pertinent information about family history (in alphabetical order): Wanda Buechler, Sandra Caulfield, Janis Cravens, Tom Loftin and Dr. Calvin McKaig. Also, gratitude is due Dorman Holub, Young County historian, for offering information and insights into the Calvin family's first years in the area; Hannah Z. Allan of the Oregon Historical Society for intriguing glimpses of the Standlee family in the late 1800s; Jennifer Bradley of the Reading Room of the Cushing Memorial Library and Archives at Texas A&M, for yearbooks and campus newspapers covering the years 1920-1924.

PUBLICATIONS

Beaumont, K.P., Brinkman, R.W., Ellis, D.R., Pourteau, J.C. and Webb, B.V., *From Anywhere to Everywhere: The Development of the Interstate Highway System in Texas* (Texas Transportation Institute, 2006).

Crouch, Carrie J., *A History of Young County, Texas* (Austin: Texas State Historical Society, 1956).

Dallek, Robert, *The Lost Peace: Leadership in a Time of Horror and Hope* (New York: Harper, 2010).

Fajardo, Luis Eduardo, "From the Alliance for Progress to the Plan Colombia: A Retrospective Look at U.S. Aid to Colombia" (London: Crisis States Programme, Development Research Centre, April 2003).

Freiberger, Steven Z., *Dawn Over Suez: The Rise of American Power in the Middle East* (Chicago: Ivan R. Dee, 1992).

Garrett, William B., "The U.S. Navy's Role in the 1956 Suez Crisis" (*Naval War College Review*, March 1970, 66-78).

Gorst, Anthony and Johnman, Lewis, *The Suez Crisis* (London and New York: Routledge, 1997).

Groves, Leslie R., *Now It Can Be Told* (New York: Da Capo Press, 1962, 1975).

Hood Panther newspaper, for details from the early days of World War II.

Kingseed, Cole C., *Eisenhower and the Suez Crisis of 1956* (Baton Rouge: LSU Press, 1995).

Kislenko, Arne, "A Not So Silent Partner: Thailand's Role in Covert Operations, Counter-Insurgency, and the Wars in Indochina" (The Journal of Conflict Studies, Summer 2004).

Levinson, Jerome, and de Onis, Juan, *The Alliance That Lost Its Way: A Critical Report on the Alliance for Progress* (New York: Quadrangle Books, 1972).

Norris, Robert S., *Racing for the Bomb: General Leslie R. Groves, the Manhattan Project's Indispensable Man* (South Royalton, VT.: Steerforth Press, 2002).

Rhodes, Richard, *The Making of the Atomic Bomb* (New York: Simon and Schuster, 25th Anniversary Edition, 2012).

Ruth, Richard A., *In Buddha's Company: Thai Soldiers in the Vietnam War* (Honolulu: University of Hawaii Press, 2011).

Swift, Earl, *The Big Roads: The Untold Story of the Engineers, Visionaries, and Trailblazers Who Created the American Superhighways* (New York: Houghton Mifflin, 2011).

Upham, Charles M., *Egyptian Highway Study,* a report to U.S. Government Foreign Operations (Cambridge, MA.: 1954).

Young County Historical Commission, *Roots in Young County* (Graham: 1978).

Two additional pieces of writing deserve special mention here: Carolyn's mother's unpublished master's thesis, *The History of Roadside Development in Texas*, and Carolyn's Aunt Mary Standlee's privately published history of Walter Reed Hospital, *Borden's Dream.*